DARK MANIPULATION

The Art of Dark Psychology, NLP Secrets, and Body Language Reading. Take Charge Using Various Mind Persuasion Techniques (202 Guide for Beginners)

Max Houle

CONTENTS

INTRODUCTION

Congratulations on your purchase of Dark Manipulation: The Art of Dark Psychology, NLP Secrets, and Body Language Reading — Thank you for Analyzing Hidden Manipulative Behavior in Relationships and Taking Control Using Different Mind Persuasion Techniques!

The world is rapidly becoming a global village, and with the need to keep up, downloading is one of the best ways to stay current. The download of the book is only the first step.

The following step should involve you reading and comprehending the information contained within it, and then actualizing it by putting it into action.

Alternatively, you can keep the information in a file and refer to it as needed. The decision is yours, but either way, you'll be glad you're well-informed.

The chapters in the book go into great detail about dark manipulation and will provide you with all of the information you will need when dealing with people who exhibit traits that are considered to be on the darker side. You will learn terms and words associated with dark psychology and gain an understanding of a branch of psychology that few have investigated.

You will learn about manipulative behaviour in relationships and even the workplace, as well as how to use various persuasion techniques for your own benefit. As a result, this book is useful in a variety of situations.

There are several books on the market on this subject, but this one will undoubtedly put you ahead of the game. Thank you for picking this book yet again! We assure you that we made every effort to prepare it.

Chapter 1
What Exactly Is Dark Psychology?

You are familiar with the term psychology; you have heard it since you were a child and know exactly what it means. Then, one day, you come across the term "dark psychology" and wonder what it means. Is it the polar opposite of psychology, and if so, what exactly does it entail? If you're looking for this information, keep reading because we'll give you juicy chunks of information that will help you understand what dark psychology is and how it works. By the end of this chapter, you should have a good understanding of what dark psychology is and what some of the terms associated with it mean. Most notably, we will discuss the "dark triad" and explain what distinguishes them from people who are considered normal in psychology. The study of the dark side of human personality is known as dark psychology. This type of research stands in stark contrast to the popular study of positive personality traits. While studying dark psychology is not the mainstream approach to psychology, it is an intriguing angle to take when approaching psychology.

Dark psychology holds that all humans are capable of predatory behaviour. We also recognise that all humans have the ability to explore their dark side and, as a result, use this ability to victimise other humans. However, few people do this, and most people are adept at restraining or sublimating these tendencies and desires. It is not uncommon to hear someone admit that they have had thoughts and feelings that they would consider brutal at some point in their lives. Dark psychology as a study seeks to understand these people's feelings, perceptions, and thoughts, as well as how their subjective processing systems work in opposition to what is considered a contemporary understanding of human behaviour. As a result, the study of dark psychology speculates that negative personality individuals' manipulation of others is usually goal-oriented and has some rationality behind it. Only a small percentage of these people would brutally victimise others without malice, and neither science nor religion can explain any of these tendencies.

- Machiavellians,
- non-clinical psychopaths,
- narcissists,
- everyday sadists

Terminology

Dark singularity: According to dark psychology, there is a region in the human psyche that allows some humans to commit atrocious acts without purpose. This is what is known as the dark singularity. Dark continuum: According to dark psychology, humans have a reservoir of malicious intent towards one another, and the acts we might want to commit in this case range from minimally intrusive acts to outright hideous psychotic and deviant behaviours for which we may lack cohesive rationality. When approaching a dark singularity, there are factors that may act as accelerants that must be considered. When these accelerants are removed and a person's heinous nature is on the dark continuum, it is referred to as the dark continuum.

The dark triad:

The dark triad in dark psychology is made up of the personality traits narcissism, psychopathy, and Machiavellianism. As previously stated, they have malevolent characteristics. Personality **Traits of People with Negative Personality Traits**

These are not ordinary people, and they frequently perplex even psychologists due to their high callousness scores, which are defined as a lack of empathy for others. As a result, they are often emotionally flat and free of remorse. They act and feel as if the world should be used to their advantage, and they use feigned emotions and high-level deception to manipulate those in their circle. They are also sociable and extroverted, which may surprise those who are unfamiliar with the dark side of human nature. However, their easygoing extroverted personality often works to their advantage because people make good first impressions, which act as a canvas for their later callous activities that make their victims' lives miserable. However, there are significant differences that distinguish these groups and have implications for the amount of damage and harm that these people can cause to people with whom they are in relationships or coworkers. The dark triad has been studied in fields such as clinical psychology, law enforcement, and business management because, interestingly, people who score high on these traits are more likely to cause social distress, commit crimes, and cause severe problems within organisations, especially when they are in positions of leadership. While their characteristics are usually distinct, some of them overlap. Each of these groups is discussed in detail below:

Narcissists

These are grandiose self-promoters who thrive on attention and are extremely proud of themselves. They also exhibit arrogance, entitlement, superiority, and dominance. Narcissism has a positive correlation with extraversion and openness and a negative correlation with agreeableness and border son psychopathy. The term narcissism is derived from the Greek myth of Narcissus, a hunter who allegedly fell in love with a reflection of himself in the water and drowned as a result. Narcissistic people are boastful, arrogant, selfish, and devoid of empathy, with a high sensitivity to criticism.

Machiavellians

The term Machiavellian is derived from the name of Niccol Machiavelli, a 16th-century Italian diplomat, and politician. "The Prince," a book written in 1513, describes Machiavelli in his official capacity as a cunning and deceitful diplomat. As a result, the characteristics associated with Machiavellianism are those that he possessed, which may include, but are not limited to, manipulation, duplicity, self-interest, and a lack of morality or emotion.

Psychopaths

The main distinguishing characteristics of psychopathy are callousness, impulsivity, and unusually bold and antisocial behaviour. They exhibit low empathy and a strong desire for thrills while making rash decisions. Some researchers have discovered a link between psychopathy and antisocial personality disorder. It has a positive relationship with extraversion and a negative relationship with agreeableness, openness, conscientiousness, and neuroticism. Identifying **Characteristics in the Dark Triad**

Psychologists have traditionally identified the traits mentioned above by measuring different personality types separately. However, in 2010, Peter Jonason, an assistant psychology professor at the University of Western Florida, and Gregory Webster, also an assistant professor, developed the Dirty Dozen rating scale. The Dark Triad Traits are measured using a 12-item scale on this scale. It is made up of questions that an individual must answer. Essentially, the person in question is rated on a scale of 1 to 7 on each of the questions, with a possible score ranging from 12 to 84 on the test. The higher a person's score, the more likely it is that they have dark triad tendencies. According to research, all three personalities in the dark triad act aggressively, are only interested in what benefits them and show no empathy or remorse. They use various techniques to manipulate and exploit people, and they are likely to violate moral values and social norms. It is suspected that these personalities are influenced by genetic factors. Because people with both personalities exhibit malicious behaviour, Machiavellianism and psychopathy are more closely related. Narcissists, on the other hand, are more fragile and defensive. This is because their arrogance and grandiosity are usually a cover-up for deeper feelings of inadequacy. Another significant difference when it comes to the dark triad is that research shows that more men than women have these personalities. This disparity is due to biological factors that make men more vulnerable, as well as social norms that allow men to cross the line. The three personality types are neither honest nor humble. When tested for cheating, studies show that all three personality types are more likely to cheat when they believe the risk of being caught is low. When their energy for thinking is low, psychopaths and Machiavellians lie and cheat, but narcissists differ because their dishonesty is primarily due to self-deception rather than intentional dishonesty.

The Dark Triad's Relationship with the Big Five Personality Test

The Big Five personality test evaluates extraversion, agreeableness, conscientiousness, openness, and neuroticism. Many people confuse agreeableness with charm and charisma. Instead, it emphasises trustworthiness, compliance, kindness, modesty, and unselfishness, all of which are positive and beneficial in interpersonal relationships. Psychopaths and Machiavellians are more likely to lack conscientiousness. Psychopaths have the lowest level of neuroticism, or the ability to feel negative emotions. It is their lack of emotions that makes them more sinister. Narcissists are the most extroverted and open of the three members of the triad. They are also open because they are imaginative.

The Dark Triad's Origins

The dark triad's origins can be difficult to explain. However, researchers are looking into the following roots for possible explanations:
• Naturalism vs. nurture
• Biological genesis
• Biological evolution

Researchers try to figure out how to understand the impact of genetic and environmental factors on different personalities. They employ twin studies in this particular case. The following is an explanation of twin studies: In each case, researchers compare the personality traits of identical twins or fraternal twins who were raised together in a similar environment. Identical twins frequently share up to 100% of their genes, whereas fraternal twins share approximately 50% of the same. It follows that, in order to aid such studies, researchers may be able to rule out genetic influence through twin studies by obtaining the correlation of identical twins and subtracting the correlation of fraternal twins. In such a case, the difference obtained usually represents half of the genetic influence. You should double the number to get the full (100 percent) genetic influence. This is known as a heritability index. Biologically, the traits have been linked to some genetic components. Researchers have also discovered that the dark triad's relationships with one another, as well as their relationships with others, are influenced by individual gene differences. Narcissism and psychopathy, in particular, are highly heritable, whereas Machiavellianism is not as heritable as the first two traits on the spectrum.

Surprisingly, when it comes to the development of negative personalities, the environment appears to account for fewer and subtler variations in individual differences. Although less subtle, this influence is still significant. In comparison to the other dark traits, Machiavellianism is more likely to be influenced by experience. This claim appears to be reasonable because there is less variance attributable to genetic factors with this trait, implying that more must be attributable to factors that are traditionally thought to be based in nature. The evolution of dark triad traits can also be explained using evolutionary theory. Evolutionary behaviour has an impact on the development of dark triad personalities and may even encourage it. When you look around, you may notice that people with dark triad traits are relatively successful. Unfortunately, this success is usually fleeting. These characteristics, according to this school of thought, emphasise mating and parenting. It is considered a fast life strategy when the emphasis is placed on mating. It is a slow-reproductive strategy when it emphasises parenting. Although some of these dark triad traits are not associated with fast life strategies, it is believed that the majority of them are. Researchers are still working to see if they can obtain more conclusive results regarding the impact of evolution on the dark triad. Fascinating facts:

1. There is scientific evidence that people with dark personalities are often judged as more attractive, especially on first impressions. This, however, should not come as a surprise to you. People with dark triad personalities, on the other hand, prefer to put extra effort into their appearance. As a result, it is likely that the difference in appearance and attractiveness disappears when these personalities are dressed casually and without make-up. The narcissists are the dark triad group most associated with this aspect.

2. The dark triad is also associated with honesty and humility. The HEXACO personality model developed the honesty-humility factor, which measures aspects of greed avoidance, fairness, sincerity, and modesty. Honesty-humility has been found to have a negative correlation with dark triad personalities, just like the big five personality test. This is understandable because these traits tend to exploit other people for personal gain, whereas the personality model in question reflects the polar opposite of such traits.

Chapter 2
Different Perspectives on the Dark Triad

The dark triad, as discussed above, may have piqued your interest, and you now want to learn more about it. If this is the case, you're on the right track. In this chapter, we learn how the members of the dark triad affect people in various ways. Most importantly, we discuss them at work, where they are common and have a negative impact on organisational outcomes.

As you proceed, it is critical to understand how critical it is to understand the effects that each of the dark personalities has on the organisation, because they each have a different impact on the organization's baseline.

The Triad of the Dark

There is a link between the dark triad and gaining leadership and interpersonal influence. We go into greater detail below:

At the office:

Machiavellianism

Many psychologists are interested in Machiavellianism in the workplace. The dark triad personalities, including Machiavellianism, have an impact on the workplace. The Machiavellianism in the workplace model consists of the following elements:

1. Power maintenance
2. Management's harsh tactics
3. Manipulative tendencies

Those who score high on the Machiavellianism spectre have high charisma levels, and their leadership is beneficial in some ways. Their presence in organisations has once again been linked to unproductive workplace behaviour.

It is widely accepted that Machiavellians are more likely to lie in interviews and are even more willing to do so. As a result, when dealing with Machiavellianism, it is unlikely that you will get honest answers in an interview. They have stronger intentions, which may lead to deception in interviews when compared to the other traits in the triad. Worse, they regard the practise of lying in interviews as acceptable.

They are likely to employ a variety of strategies to sway the interviewers in their favour. Men who practise Machiavellianism are more likely to make up information about themselves in an interview and give their interviewers the least amount of freedom to direct content in an interview.

Machiavellians are also known to be manipulative and exploitative in the workplace in order to advance their own personal agendas and maintain their dominance over others.

This group of people's guiding beliefs are as follows:
* Never show humility.
* Dealing with arrogance with others is more effective; ethics and morality are not and will never be part of them.

These are taken into account for the week. They have the right to lie, cheat, and deceive as they see fit.

* They prefer to be feared rather than loved by others.
* failing to share important information;
* spreading false rumours about a coworker;
* failing to meet work obligations; and making others look bad in subtle ways in front of management.

As a result, studies show that there is a link between workplace bullying and Machiavellianism. Bullying is thus negatively correlated with perceptions of adhocracy and more positively with perceptions of hierarchy culture. This concept was also associated with abusive subordinate supervision.

Narcissism

Narcissism in the workplace is harmful to an organisation because these individuals are more likely to engage in counterproductive work behaviour when their self-esteem is threatened. This characteristic is also a personality disorder.

These triad members typically perform well in job interviews, resulting in higher hiring ratings than their normal counterparts. Even trained and experienced raters may fail to notice the depth of their deception. It is speculated that one of the reasons they may receive higher ratings is that interviews are different from other social situations. Consider the following:

In an interview, you are permitted to brag in order to make a good impression.

Narcissists use this as an opportunity to outperform their coworkers.

These individuals are highly skilled at displaying cues that make them likeable, which allows them to make positive impressions even when they do not intend to maintain a high level of job performance in the long run. As a result, it is likely that when you first meet a narcissist at work, you will identify with them as agreeable, well-adjusted, competent, and entertaining. They dress neatly and flashily, make confident body movements, and have friendly facial expressions. Unfortunately, such good news for them is always fleeting, as soon as interest in them begins to wane.

Organizational stress, absenteeism, and staff turnover are all influenced by narcissists. People who work and interact with narcissists experience a high level of stress. Interpersonal aggression, sabotaging others' work, and wasting other people's time and energy are all associated with narcissism. Employees' stress levels rise as a result of such counterproductive workplace procedures, resulting in staff absenteeism and high staff turnover rates.

Narcissists must have a steady supply in order to thrive. A narcissistic manager, for example, will have an inanimate and animate supply that will tolerate his narcissistic behaviour. Inanimate attention supplies include gadgets, office views, and cars, whereas animate attention supplies include coworkers and colleagues. Sometimes teammates will offer assistance, only to discover that if proper boundaries are not maintained, these offers will turn them into a constant supply. A narcissistic manager will frequently shield his supply networks from objective decision-making. Such managers frequently evaluate the benefits of long-term strategies based on the amount of gain they will receive rather than the benefit to the organisation.

Furthermore, narcissistic people prefer hierarchical organisations because they see it as a way to advance to higher ranks and gain benefits such as power and status. They are eager to advance to the highest levels of an organisation and are ultimately more successful in doing so. As a result, you won't find them in a setting where opportunities for advancement are slim. They will be more concerned with how they are perceived and whether or not they are praised than with what benefits the stakeholders. While some narcissistic traits may be advantageous, not enough research has been conducted to determine how narcissism affects an organisation.

Corporate narcissism can occur at times. This occurs when a narcissist rises through the ranks and becomes a member of senior management, a CEO, or is in a leadership role that allows them to gather an adequate mix of co-dependents who provide him with the attention he requires as a narcissist.

They may profess to care about the company, but in reality, they are only interested in their own agendas.

This is why such people can run financially successful businesses while adhering to unhealthy principles. To distinguish a good organisation from a pathological one, consider an organization's ability to exclude narcissists from positions of power.

When it comes to workplace bullying, narcissists prefer to use indirect methods such as ignoring a person, withholding critical information that may affect a person's performance, constantly reminding someone of their mistakes, spreading malicious information, and assigning work that is below a person's competency levels.

They prefer indirect methods such as threatening, yelling, falsely accusing, and criticising employees. Because they have low self-esteem, narcissists are more likely to be aggressive and confrontational. When they bully someone, they usually feel a sense of accomplishment after the incident. They generally avoid work but are not afraid of stealing someone else's work in any way.

They are also manipulative, as you are probably aware of the triad by now, and will frequently manipulate within the work environment in order to take credit for accomplishments within the organisation to which they did not contribute.

Psychopathy

Surprisingly, only a small percentage of the workforce is present. However, they should not be underestimated because, even in small numbers, psychopaths can cause irreversible damage to a company or organisation, particularly when in senior management positions. They are, paradoxically, more common at higher levels of organisations, where they have the ability and power to reign terror, and the ripple effects are felt throughout the organisation. As a result, their actions usually have a way of influencing a company's corporate culture, and of course, it will be a poor culture that does not consider the feelings of its employees. Some of the consequences of psychopaths' actions within organisations.

Psychopaths in the workplace alter their personalities to meet their needs. They may, for example, be charming to those above their level in a hierarchy while being abusive to those below them in the organisation. As a result, they present various versions of themselves to different staff members. There are some distinctions between psychopaths. There are successful psychopaths, for example, who are corporate and engage in illegal activities. They most likely come from privileged backgrounds with little risk of punishment, as well as a high IQ, which provides a foundation for successful psychopathy. On the other end of the spectrum is the unsuccessful psychopath who engages in regular crime, has a low IQ, and thus faces a high penalty risk.

Here's something you should know:

According to the clinical criteria, up to 1% of the general population can be classified as psychopathic. Furthermore, psychopaths are more prevalent in the business world than in the general population, particularly in senior positions. Lawyers, those in the media, journalists, police officers, cooks, clergy, and surgeons are also likely members of this dark triad.

Following that, we'll look at the Organizational Psychopath.

Typically, these people want to be almost like gods, having power over others and preferring to work at the highest levels of the organisation. They prefer this type of work arrangement because, as previously stated, it allows them to control the greatest number of people. Political leaders, CEOs, and managers are all examples of people who fall into this category.

When they communicate, they appear intelligent, charming, witty, and sometimes sincere, as well as entertaining. They are quick to analyse what someone wants and then create a narrative that fits the person's expectations. They usually coerce people into doing what they want, including their work, and take credit for the work of others while delegating their own responsibilities to junior staff members. When it comes to dealing with others, they have a low tolerance level and only show shallow emotions. They're just as unpredictable, and you can't count on them to keep their end of the bargain. Furthermore, they cannot be relied on to accept full responsibility when something goes wrong.

As a result, psychopaths have an advantage when working in organisations that have been overrun by abusive supervision because they are more stress-resistant and can put up with interpersonal abuse while ignoring the need for positive relationships among coworkers.

Psychopaths advance through the career ladder and learn to maintain power in the stages outlined below:

• **Entry:** Because of their highly developed social skills, psychopaths can easily obtain employment within organisations. It will be difficult for anyone to notice their psychopathic tendencies at this stage due to their charm and quick wit. Indeed, if you have one in your workplace, you may recall them as benevolent or helpful.

• **Assessment:** During the assessment, the typical psychopath will weigh you on a scale to determine how useful you are to him. You are either a patron or a pawn at this point. Patrons are like gods, meant to be pleased because of their formal power and need for protection in the game. Pawns are manipulated for their own personal gain, whereas pawns are manipulated for their own personal gain.

• **Manipulation:** At this stage, the psychopath conjures up a psychopathic fiction scenario in which they create perceptions about themselves and others. As a result, other people will be shown with negative disinformation, while they will be shown in a positive light. They will groom you as a pawn in his network and will coerce you into accepting their agenda without your knowledge.

• **Confrontation:** Typically, the psychopath will assassinate your character and that of others during this stage in order to keep the agenda that they forced you to accept in the first stage. This is how you get to be a pawn or a patron.

• **Ascension:** As they rise through the ranks, one of the patrons he/she values must be eliminated in order for him to assume a position of power and prestige. It's worth noting that this occurs at the expense of someone who once supported them.

If you pay close attention to trends, you may have noticed that organisations frequently hire psychopaths. This phenomenon is harmful. However, here's why it happens:

Most job descriptions tend to attract psychopaths because they demonstrate that companies have an innate desire to engage with people who are willing to go to any length to succeed, even if it means putting others first. In some cases, advertisements directly target these people. Furthermore, they are being recruited to organisations because of their charm and ability to make positive first impressions—they are appealing to those hiring because they have the tendency to appear well emotionally adjusted, reasonable, and easy to get along with, which are some of the other qualities that the panel seeks.

Furthermore, their irresponsibility comes across in such a way that even skilled interviewers may misinterpret it as risk-taking and entrepreneurial.

Their desire for thrills, on the other hand, may be misinterpreted as enthusiasm for the job, and managers may sometimes encourage their efforts. Their charm is mistaken for charisma, laying the groundwork for long-term disaster.

Finally, they are likely to falsify their educational accomplishments, such as awards, degrees, and diplomas, in order to appear more qualified.

Psychopaths are sometimes promoted because they are polished, charming, cool, and decisive. Furthermore, they benefit from their manipulative and bullying abilities. They use their power to divide and rule before ascending the corporate ladder and promoting their own agenda.

The Internet

People who are internet trolls have been found to have dark personality traits. They exhibit sadism, Machiavellianism, psychopathy, and antisocial behaviour as a result.

Cyberbullying is the deliberate and persistent bullying of someone on the internet. Because it is usually anonymous, the experience can be harrowing and psychologically unsettling. This attack mode has become a popular choice for many people today, as even young people engage in cyberbullying behaviour that threatens and degrades others.

• Posting pictures that can be altered and shared on websites, especially when relationships are strained.

• Creating online bulletin boards and bash boards that contribute to bashful and hateful text wars between two or more parties (the intended party may end up receiving folds of cruel messages every day; these victims frequently become victims of negative emotional effects).

What makes cyberbullying particularly effective on victims is that, unlike traditional forms of bullying, they usually do not know the identity of their abuser. Indirect aggression is the name given to this type of attack. People with dark personalities prefer this platform because they are more comfortable saying things to their counterparts online than they are in person. Even in a traditional setting, it is clear that the bullying was planned and intentional. The main reasons they engage in such acts may include retaliation and softening their victims when they believe they are resisting their efforts. Because this method of attack is non-confrontational, bullies may prefer it because it gives them a sense of security while remaining anonymous.

Psychopathy is the trait most closely associated with both types of bullying, followed by Machiavellianism and finally bullying.

Managing the Dark Triad at Work

To conclude this chapter, we will discuss some of the techniques you can use at work to deal with each personality in the dark triad. If you work with a narcissist, Machiavellian, or psychopath, keep reading:

Narcissists

We've already established that narcissists can make life difficult at work. The worst part is that you have no control over the settings themselves. All you have to do is work around them.

To ensure that these steps are worthwhile, examine the organisation and ensure that it does not reinforce narcissistic tendencies by rewarding narcissists with promotions and raises. If the organisation encourages these tendencies in any way, you may need to look for a new job. If not, follow the steps outlined below:

Ensure that everything is documented. If instructions are given verbally at your workplace, you can make a formal request to have them emailed to you instead. This way, you'll have documentation of what the narcissist said and when. You can also write down what they say and go over it with them to ensure accuracy upon review. You don't leave anything to chance when you have this kind of personality. Document events, times, dates, and verbatim quotes because they may be useful later, especially if you need to consult with an attorney.

✓ Avoidance is yet another tactic for dealing with narcissists. As a member of the dark triad, they are constantly looking for ways to bring you down at work. You should avoid giving them any opportunities at all costs because they will do everything in their power to find and exploit your weaknesses. For example, they may use your family to get to you by making snide remarks when you are not on good terms with them. In this case, the comments may imply, for example, that you are not a good mother, especially if your coworkers know how important family life is to you. Normally, if a comment like this is made, it has nothing to do with the situation at hand, and you should recognise it as the classic narcissist seeking you out in a game where they will finish you as they see fit. They understand that using your family role against you is the ultimate way to detonate you. When this occurs, avoid engaging in conversation with them. Keep in mind that this is the personality of the narcissist, and it has nothing to do with you. Despite the urge to fight back, take a step back and walk away without saying anything. This will not only make them wonder what you think, but it will also make them doubt their own ability to take control of situations. As previously stated, document everything in such cases and keep details such as dates, locations, and quotes in mind.

Also, you must recognise that a narcissist's choice of you as their target is deliberate, but that the entire scenario is not personal. Even if you are the victim of a narcissist, it is usually not because you have done something wrong, but because you are doing better than them in some way.

The narcissist, you see, despises anyone who is thought to be doing better than him and will seek you out not because of any crime, but because of them and the deep insecurity, they feel within themselves. What may perplex people who find themselves entangled with narcissists at work is that they frequently appear to have it all together. When you realise that their battles aren't personal, you realise that walking away is not only possible, but also more rewarding than engaging with a narcissist.

✓ Avoid giving the workplace narcissist your opinions or personal information, as this will expose you to their criticism. You must understand that narcissists are experts at soliciting the opinions of others. When you turn your back, the narcissist will stab you with even the most trivial of opinions. For example, if he asks what you think of a four-person team, you may simply say that you think the team is great, but Sally could have done well in Reinhardt's team. While this is a common remark, the narcissist can wait until your relationship with Sally is not going well to use this information to divide and rule. He could simply say that you told Sally she wasn't good enough for her team. This is how narcissists survive: they twist other people's words. It is therefore your responsibility to figure out what strategy the narcissist is employing and to refrain from engaging him. When asked for personal opinions, change direction by walking away or changing the subject—no matter what the circumstances—do not give the narcissist a foothold. It is not uncommon to hear the workplace narcissist approaching you and claiming to want to meet with you privately.

If this occurs, consider having someone else accompany you as a witness. Having a witness works in your favour in two ways. First, having a witness can deter a narcissist from saying something that they know could cause disruption, and second, if they tell a lie about you or that interaction in the future, the witness can then act in your defence because they witnessed the events that occurred.

If you want to thrive in an organisation with a narcissist, avoid contact. This advice may appear simple, but it can be one of the most difficult to implement. Every cloud, however, has a silver lining. The silver lining in this scenario is that this tactic almost always works. Narcissists panic when you refuse to play their games and instead choose an alternative method. If you have to interact with the narcissist on a regular basis because you work together, keep it to basic facts. As previously stated, do not be tempted to express your opinion. If you work in the same building and feel you can no longer work with the narcissist, you can arrange and request a different position within the same building. Most importantly, make sure you understand your legal rights.

You must understand that narcissists are astute individuals.

You will notice that the narcissist will irritate you just enough to make you angry, but they will not engage in the illegal practice. They, therefore, understand what they are doing. However, due to their self-pleasing nature, they commonly cross the border, and sooner or later, they cross the line. This is why it is important to understand the role you play in an organisation and the rights you have, especially if it is a narcissistic manager. The Equal Employment Opportunity Commission in the United States, for example, states that you should not be treated differently or be discriminated based on gender, age, nationality, or creed. Also, the employer has a duty to ensure that the employees work in a conducive environment so that they do not become part of an intolerable environment in which they cannot survive. Apart from discrimination, the law also protects you from harassment and from being harassed if you report your employer. It is, therefore, up to you to decide how far you would like to make a case against your narcissistic superior at work.

Psychopaths

Working with a psychopath can be harmful to your mental health and generally toxic. A psychopath in the workplace may not pose a physical threat to you, but there is a significant emotional risk in entertaining a psychopath in the workplace. Take the following steps to help mitigate the damage:

Keep your emotions under control. Imagine wanting to cry or yell at someone who is grating on your nerves, but being unable to do so. It sounds exasperating. However, when there is a psychopath in the picture, you must sometimes do the unexpected. Keeping your emotions under control sends a message to the psychopath that they have no control over you. When you react predictably and lose your cool, you massage the ego of the psychopath, who realises they have power over you and can easily manipulate you with emotions. This scenario can be aggravating, especially at work. As a result, the best action you can take is to present yourself as calmly as possible at all times.

✓ Don't tell them you're scared of them. As previously stated, psychopaths use a variety of intimidation tactics on their victims. They intimidate you by standing over you while you talk, using aggressive language to prevent you from expressing yourself, and making subtle threats. When this happens, many people back down and succumb to the psychopath's ideas and impulsions.

✓ Also, make certain that you do not believe their stories. This member of the triad has a tendency to tell stories that portray them as victims. However, you will discover that these stories are always false, and it is simply a case of them refusing to accept responsibility for their actions. When you listen to their longwinded stories, you enable and validate them.

When having discussions, stick to the facts when and if necessary. There is also a technique that can be used to disarm psychopaths. Pointing out their own flaws usually disarms them because it demonstrates that someone understands their tricks and can point them out. For example, if they start telling stories about how they are victimising themselves again, interrupt and ask them if they are okay. Inquire about a specific incident that occurred during the morning meeting. When you do this, they see that you are not interested in their fabricated stories and realise that you have blown their cover, making it difficult for you to continue being a victim of his schemes. Communicate via the internet. Because there are no written records, these people can sometimes get away with their lies and deception. They take advantage of the fact that there are no written records to back up their claims.

Furthermore, a psychopath is more likely to excel at negotiation when speaking face to face because they have mastered the art of manipulation and can simply charm their way into a deal. Ensuring that you communicate online is a good way to disarm them because the chances of them charming their way through conversation and getting a good deal are low. Ensure that your request for all conversations to take place online is granted, and work on your mental fortitude. Working with a psychopath can have mental consequences you never imagined. As a result, it is critical that you learn to exercise your mental muscles. You can effectively accomplish this by taking a proactive approach to stress management. You may find yourself struggling with your mental health, and this is a good time to seek the assistance of a mental health professional who will work with you to find solutions to your problems. You may believe you have everything under control, but remember that even the strongest can crumble, and working with someone who exhibits toxic traits may affect you as well.

✓ Understand your rights in case they go too far.

Sometimes people suffer within an organisation because they are dealing with a psychopath, but no one knows about it, and those who do know don't know how to deal with it because they are usually in top management. Many countries have laws that protect their citizens from workplace harassment and discrimination. It may thus be beneficial to keep your records straight if he/she goes unchecked. If you decide to report the incident, know that the law protects you from further harassment and that you will most likely have taken a step that will save the company, stakeholders, and other employees who may be experiencing the same thing but are unable to speak up.

Dealing with a psychopath is difficult because they are often successful personalities who are well placed in the corporate ladder and use their power to bully, intimidate, and suppress other employees. If the proper steps are taken, you have a chance of avoiding an emotional rollercoaster for yourself and your coworkers.

Machiavellians

Machiavellians go to great lengths to maintain their power, and as a result, they are manipulative and lack empathy. They are only concerned with what will benefit them. Dealing with a Machiavellian can be difficult because they can sometimes unleash their acts so subtly that they are difficult to detect. This is not to say that you should give up hope. Here are some strategies for dealing with them:

Ascertain that they are, in fact, Machiavellian in nature. You do not want to make incorrect accusations because treading these paths can be hazardous. However, it may be beneficial for you to understand which of the dark triad personalities the person you are dealing with belongs to. If they are manipulative at work and will go to any length to get where they want to go, they exhibit classic Machiavellianism. To confirm this, look for patterns that show that the person does those things on a consistent basis. There may be isolated incidents where a staff member or manager is simply looking out for themselves. This does not imply that they are Machiavellian in any way. If the patterns are consistent, your guess is as good as ours: they are fundamentally Machiavellian.

✓ If you are in a position, address the employee; if you are in a lower position of power, seek assistance in dealing with the Machiavellian. You must proceed with caution because these personalities are difficult to deal with, and you may end up triggering a situation that becomes even more difficult. When approaching this dark triad personality, it is best to approach them when they are in a gay mood. When you do, be truthful. Inform them of the consequences of their actions on those around them. Give them specific examples to back up what you're saying to help them feel the gravity of the situation.

Inform them that it would be beneficial to everyone if they could change their ways and that not changing their ways could have a negative impact on the entire organisation.

✓ Determine what sets off the Machiavellian response. There is a chance that your Machiavellian will respond rationally to the claims made against them. However, at this point, it is critical to exercise caution. You can work with them to figure out what their triggers are. Are there situations, for example, that cause their dark trait to emerge?

✓ A scenario like this could work. You may notice that the Machiavellian trait emerges when they work with a particular coworker or see a specific manager. While it is not advisable to shrink yourself to fit the expectations of another at work, it is prudent to separate the two. In fact, it may be beneficial to refrain from collaborating. This step is most effective when performed by management rather than coworkers.

✓ Do not condone their actions. Machiavellians do not require others to condone their bad behaviour. As a result, do not entertain them in any capacity, whether as a coworker or as a manager. Subtly thwart their efforts whenever possible. Do not make excuses for them or defend them when they are wrong and do not fall victim to their deception. If other staff members discover that you are supporting a Machiavellian at their expense, you may find yourself alone and without friends, especially if the Machiavellian decides to dispose of you.

The following exclusive tips may be useful for those in management:

When hiring, look for Machiavellian characteristics. The hiring team is frequently so taken with the Machiavellian's display of all the right characteristics that they fail to see past their make-believe mask. However, the simplest and most effective way to eliminate these types of employees from the workplace is to not hire them in the first place. We understand that identifying Machiavellian tendencies in a short time span such as an interview can be difficult, but we would recommend using an industrial psychologist, and if you cannot use a professional, then weed out a candidate who you believe has Machiavellian or dark triad traits as soon as possible. The interview process can also include various activities that reveal more about a job candidate's characteristics before they are hired.

✓ Stick to your guns with the Machiavellian. Sometimes you'll discover that your team already has a Machiavellian on its team. They've also already got their talons on their prize, and everyone in the office seems to like them for the time being. You feel excluded because you are the only one who can see through their charade, and you are unsure what to do about it.

There is an old adage that if you can't beat them, at least join them. Don't fall for it. Instead, stand your ground; as a manager, you are in charge and should act accordingly. Do not be swayed or wooed by their antics, and do not allow these toxic behaviours to continue, as they will have an impact on how the company performs over time, with serious consequences for everyone, not just the employees.

Maintain your composure. It's important to stand your ground, but it's even more important to maintain your cool when dealing with the Machiavellian. They are usually malicious and are only waiting for you to make a mistake before making their move. They may not mind portraying you as an emotional wreck and supporting it with evidence of how you once flew off the handle when something happened because they are deceptive. And yet, dealing with dark triad traits is difficult because they tend to make you emotional. It won't be easy, but being rational is the only way to ensure that the Machiavellian doesn't beat you at your own game.

Only cut cords when absolutely necessary. Even after attempting the aforementioned remedies, you may notice that the employee has not changed significantly. This behaviour will have an impact on the company over time, as other employees will be discouraged.

When such behaviour goes unpunished or unaddressed, it is natural for office morale to suffer. You should consider terminating your working relationship with the Machiavellian at this point. Be cautious here because, according to the law, you need a legitimate reason to fire someone in most places, and some of these personalities are so careful to only commit crimes within the law. What can work in your favour is that the dark personalities are so self-absorbed that they sometimes make firing-worthy mistakes. Just keep an eye out for it and seize the opportunity when you see it.

Chapter 3
NLP Secrets and Reading Body Language

NLP is an abbreviation for neuro-linguistic programming. Many people have heard of it, but they are unsure what it is. The good news is that there is always a right time to learn—and that time is now. Continue reading to learn what NLP is and how it relates to body language.

We will also teach you how to read body language to help you understand what someone is thinking.

What Exactly Is Neuro-Linguistic Programming (NLP) Therapy?

NLP is a technique for personal development, psychotherapy, and even communication. In the 1970s, two people, John Grinder and Richard Bandler, came up with the idea. Bandler was a mathematician and information scientist, while Grinder was a linguist. Leslie Cameron Bandler, Judith DeLozier, David Gordon, and Robert Dilts also contributed to the concept.

In their book," Structure of Magic: A Book about Language of Therapy released in 1975, attempted to highlight communication patterns that set excellent communicators from the not-so-excellent ones. The work in this book was based on the works of Milton Erickson, Fritz Perls, and Virginia Satir. The book also had important information regarding theories and techniques from renowned professionals and researchers, including Noam Chomsky, Carlos Castaneda, Alfred Korzybski, and Gregory Bateson. In the end, they developed the NLP meta-model.

The name neurolinguistic means that as the creators of the concept believe there is a connection between neurological processes, language, and behaviour patterns that are learned through experience. They believe that programming can be changed to achieve some goals in life. Grinder and Bandler say that the NLP technique can model the behaviour and skills of an exceptional person.

This technique may also appeal to you if you have phobias, tic disorders, depression, allergy, near-sightedness, learning disorders, and psychosomatic illnesses. There was a growing interest in this approach towards the end of the 70s because the two authors started marketing it as a tool that could help individuals achieve success. It is no wonder that NLP has been adopted by hypnotherapists and companies that use leadership training as a tool for improving business and government agencies. To this end, it is used in fields including but not limited to medicine, law, counseling, business, sports, performing arts, military, and education.

As such, this concept incorporates sensory and language-based interventions together with behaviour modification techniques to help improve the communication skills, confidence, and self-awareness of an individual. The belief is that one individual, usually the therapist, can understand the way another accomplishes a task and so help them copy and communicate this information to others so that they too can accomplish a given task. The goals of NLP are, therefore, to help the client understand their views of the world and how it affects how they operate and lets them know that it is necessary to change behavior patterns and thoughts for better outcomes. The concept is meant to help change patterns that have proven not beneficial in the past.

Core Concepts and Components of the NLP Technique

In NLP, there are three main components and central components crucial for its understanding. They include:

• **Subjectivity.** Grinder and Bandler suppose that the world is experienced subjectively by us, it, therefore, follows that humans create a subjective representation for each experience that they have. The experienced are constituted in the five senses that we have and in language. Our conscious experience is, therefore, in terms of smell, touch, sight, taste, \sand hearing when we think about an activity that we will carry out in the future, we anticipate what it will feel like and the tastes, sounds, and flavours that we will experience. According to the theory, these subjective representations follow a discernible pattern/structure. As such, euro-linguistic programming is usually described as the study of subjective experience's structure. The behaviour of a person can be understood and described based on these sense-based subjective representations. Behavior can either be verbal or nonverbal, adaptive or maladaptive, competent or incompetent and skillful or ineffective. Your behaviour and that of others can be modified.

• **Consciousness** The knowledge that conscious as a component is divided into the conscious and unconscious is the foundation of Neuro-Linguistic Programming. Subjective representations can occur outside of an individual's awareness and constitute what is known as the unconscious mind.

• **Education.** Modeling, an imitative learning method, is used in Neuro-Linguistic programming. Modeling is the process of codifying and reproducing a person's experiences in any domain of activity. The description of the sequence of the linguistic and sensory representations of the example's subjective experience during execution is an important part of the coding process.

When Is Neuro-Linguistic Programming Therapy Administered, and What Can You Expect?

As previously stated, neuro-linguistic therapy has been used to treat negative psychological issues. It is used to combat the majority of these issues because they tend to lower overall quality of life.

If you've made it this far, you deserve to know what to expect when neuro-linguistic programming is used. Some of the techniques used in NLP therapy are described below:

• **Visualization:** Creating a mental image of something with the assistance of a therapist.

• **Visual kinesthetic dissociation:** being guided by the therapist to revisit past traumatic events so that the victim can live out the experience from afar, in an imaginative out-of-body manner.

The therapist can use these techniques to access his patient's past and correct faulty language, which leads to faulty communication and negative thinking. Depending on the scope of the problem and the victim, these techniques can be used in both the short and long term. The underlying assumption is that all human action is positive. As a result, if a plan fails or when the unexpected occurs, there is no good or bad outcome. This experience, on the other hand, can be a source of useful information that can be used to better understand life.

The therapist uses neuro-linguistic programming techniques to assist the client in understanding his own minds and how they came to be in the state in which they operate—how they communicate, think, and behave. They can also manage their moods and emotions, and they can easily reprogram their information processing abilities, resulting in more acceptable behaviour that can be used to get what they want in their immediate environment. Simultaneously, neuro-linguistic programming is a tool that recognises the ways in which patients have previously been successful in order to assist them in determining how they can efficiently repeat their success stories in other aspects and areas of life. As a result, NLP therapists believe that you, the client, have all of the answers within you. Their job is to assist you in getting the answers you need in the most efficient way possible.

Neuro-Linguistic Programming Practice Sets

An interaction in neuro-linguistic programming can be thought of as a series of stages that include establishing a rapport, gathering information about a problem, the mental state of the person, and the goals desired by the person, then using specific techniques and tools to make interventions, and finally integrating these proposed solutions into the client's life. The client's nonverbal responses usually guide the entire process.

1. Pacing and leading the verbal, for example, through keywords and sensory predicates, as well as nonverbal behaviour, such as matching the nonverbal behaviour and responding to the client's eye movements, are used to establish and maintain rapport.

2. Information gathering occurs after rapport is established. At this point, the practitioner collects information from the client by asking meta-model questions. During the interaction, which follows the description of the client's current state, these questions are meant to reveal a lot about the client's desired goal.

3. When defining the client's current and desired states, as well as the resources that may be required to bridge the gap, special attention is paid to the client's verbal and nonverbal cues. During this time, the practitioner encourages them to consider the implications of the desired outcome and how these implications may affect his relationships, personal or professional life. They conduct an ecological assessment of any potential problems. An ecological check is essentially a set of positive intentions that arise as a result of a problem.

4. The fourth stage entails the practitioner assisting the client in achieving the desired outcomes through the use of tools and techniques that will change internal representations of the stimuli they encounter in the real world into their lives. At this point, the practitioner may, for example, ask the client to imagine themselves in the future and describe or represent, using their senses, how they will feel after achieving the desired outcome.

Neuro-linguistic programming, according to researchers, also involves outlying discourse analysis and provides a practical outline that works to ensure better communication. Some researchers, for example, believe that when you use the word but, people remember what you said after you say it. However, if you use and, what you said before and after is more likely to be remembered. As a result, positivity is essential in language and how it is decoded.

How the Method Works

Modeling, action, and effective communication are key components of neuro-linguistic programming. According to the model's adherents, everyone has a personal map of what they consider reality. As a result, a person who practises NLP analyses their own perspective as well as the perspectives of others to create what is known as a systematic overview of a single situation. A user of the neuro-linguistic programming technique gains information by understanding different points of view. It is also believed that the senses play an important role in information processing. As a result, the body and mind interact with one another. This is a hands-on approach. So, if a person wants to understand an action, he must participate in it so that it becomes an experience from which they can learn. There are hierarchies of learning, change, and communication, according to NLP practitioners. The following are the levels of change:

- **Purpose and spirituality:** This is where one feels a sense of belonging to something bigger than themselves. This can include ethics, religion, and other belief systems. This level represents the greatest amount of change.

- **Identity:** This is the person you believe you are. The scope of identity is broad and may include your life roles and responsibilities.

- **Beliefs and values** This level includes the things that are important to you and your beliefs.

- **Competencies and abilities**. This level encompasses everything you can do and all of your abilities.

- **Behaviours:** these are the specific actions you take.

- **Environment:** The environment is the most basic level of change and includes you, your surroundings, and the context or setting.

The goal of each of these logical levels is to organise and direct the information that lies beneath it. As a result, changes made at the lower levels may cause changes at the higher levels. Changes at the higher levels frequently result in changes at the lower levels.

NLP in the Therapy Setting

In therapy, NLP holds that reality and belief are frequently at odds.

As such, as a person, you operate and see things from your own perspective rather than from objectivity. As such, the beliefs of everyone in the world are limited, distorted, unique, or a mixture of both. If therefore, a therapist is supposed to treat a patient, then they have to understand the map perception of the individual they are dealing with as this perception may have a bearing on how the person views the world.

The data received through the senses will then be used to form the individual's perception map. Senses include sight, touch, smell, and taste, and as such, information can come in through any of the senses. The difference in information occurs on the basis of quality and importance, and each person receives their information through a primary representational system. For the therapy to be successful, the therapist must try to match the patient's primary representational system so that they can use their map to help them navigate a situation. Neuro-linguistic programming practitioners believe that you can access the primary representational system using cues such as eye movements. By doing such, they are able to understand the thinking and behavioural patterns of these individuals.

Supporters of this approach claim that it produces fast and longlasting results that are effective at improving understanding of behavioral and cognitive patterns. The NLP approach also builds effective communication between the conscious and unconscious mind and their processes and thus, is an important way through which the individual can improve creativity and problem-solving skills.

Primarily, this method is compared to cognitive behavioural therapy, but the adherents insist that these positive changes can be made with neuro-linguistic programming in short amounts of time.

Applications of the Neuro-Linguistic Programming Technique in Today's World

Neuro-linguistic programming has come a long way since the 1970s. Today, it is applied in a wide array of fields and in different ways. Below we explore some of the ways in which NLP is applied:

• **In alternative medicine:** Alternative medicine is an evergreen field that integrates various techniques to ensure positive outcomes for clients. Over time, NLP has been used as a tool in alternative medicine that can be used in the treatment of diseases such as Parkinson's and even cancer. However, it is important to realise that there is no medical evidence that can back up these claims. Resorting to neuro-linguistic programming in such serious cases can, therefore, result in negative health consequences. In order to ensure that you fully understand the range of applications for NLP and to understand where you should place your boundaries, it is important to read the next section as we explain the evolution of research about neuro-linguistic programming.

- **In psychotherapy:** The early models of the neuro-linguistic programming technique were psychotherapists. This means that the early NLP books had a psycho-therapeutic focus.

When viewed as an approach to psychotherapy, the technique shares the same core foundations and assumptions as some contemporary systematic and brief practices. Neurolinguistic programming has also affected some practices, especially with the reframing techniques that it employs to change behaviour by shifting the context or meaning for the client. There are two main therapeutic uses of neuro-linguistic programming including as a specific therapy, in which case it is referred to as neuro-linguistic therapy and as an aide-de-camp to therapists who use it together with other therapeutic techniques within the discipline.

Neurolinguistic psychotherapy is recognised in the United Kingdom by the United Kingdom Council for Psychotherapy. At first, accreditation was governed by Association for Neuro-Linguistic programming and later by Neuro-Linguistic Psychotherapy and Counselling Association. However, neuro-linguistic psychotherapy and neuro-linguistic programming are both not approved by NICE in the United Kingdom.

Neuro-linguistic programming shares a similarity with Scientology and Citizens Commission on Human Rights. This is especially true when you look at the range of physical and mental conditions that the technique is believed to cure. According to Bandler and Grinder, NLP can cure dyslexia, myopia ad epilepsy and can be a pathway towards recovery in the treatment of schizophrenia, depression, and PTSD. It also dismisses psychiatric illnesses as psychosomatic much like Scientology does. However, as is revealed below, research shows that there is little to no connection between NLP intervention and the improvement of health-related outcomes.

Other uses. Originally, the use of neuro-linguistic programming was mainly therapeutic. Today, however, the generic nature of the practice allowed it to be practised in a variety of other fields and is applied differently, for example in persuasion, negotiation & sales, training of management, team building, teaching, coaching, and public speaking.

NLP in Research

In the late 70s, the concept of neuro-linguistic programming begun to crop up, it was valued as a communication study and as a business tool. Over time, students and psychotherapists have begun to form around the initial works of Grinder and Bandler, which spread the theory and practise of NLP. Some prominent figures of the time, such as Tony Robbins, trained with one of the authors, Grinder and used NLP philosophies in his motivational and self-help programs.

The use of NLP begun to spread among practitioners and theorists, making it less uniform than it was during its inception. Soon, scientists were empirically testing the scientific underpinnings of the theory, and the research indicated a lack of empirical support for its essential theories. Over time, the decline in debate saw a decline in the number of studies around neuro-linguistic programming.

However, in the recent past, there have been several studies that have redirected their focus to NLP.

Some research has been carried out with the intention of investigating how effective NLP is as a treatment method. A 2013 research revealed that the visualisation techniques employed in NLP could be helpful for children with special needs within the classroom environment. These techniques could be helpful in preparing them for classroom learning as they helped the children develop a positive mindset to learning. However, the results are yet to be ascertained because it used a minimal sample of only seven children, the findings are, therefore, classified as tentative conclusions that may need further investigation.

NLP therapists have long held the belief that eye movement is a reliable lie detection indicator. A research was carried out in 2012 in a set of three studies to ascertain how well established this claim was and how true it stands in today's world. The first study challenged the neuro-linguistic eye movement hypothesis when it revealed that the eye movements when a participant was telling the truth or lying did not match the hypothesis. The second study involved two groups.

One group was told about the NLP eye movement hypothesis while the second remained ignorant as they were not told anything about the hypothesis. The study revealed that there were no differences between the two groups after the lie detection test. The third study involved the coding of eye movements of two distinct groups at a public conference. There was no significant difference in eye movement recorded in the two groups as well, disapproving the NLP eye movement hypothesis.

Additionally, in 2012, a systematic review of literature on the impact of neuro-linguistic programming on health was conducted. The studies reviewed covered a wide range of issues—including anxiety, morning sickness, weight management, claustrophobia, and substance abuse—were analyzed. The researchers found that there was no significant evidence that suggested that NLP could actually improve health. However, there was no evidence that suggested that NLP was ineffective either. The choice is, therefore, left for you to make as to whether you want to explore an area of NLP or not.

As a Quasi-Religion, Neuro-Linguistic Programming

Some anthropologists and sociologists consider NLP as a quasi-religion of the new age and classify it as a part of the Human Potential Movement instead of seeing it as a science. They believe that NLP is a practise that embraces symbolic efficiency rather than physical efficiency, which makes it able to effect change through a placebo effect. NLP is therefore parallel to syncretic folk religion and attempts to marry aspects of professional medicine to the magic of practicing folklore. This may be true because both Bandler and Grinder were followers of Shamanism and several of their ideas have been borrowed from Shamanism and incorporated into NLP. Some of these ideas include the notion of the stopping world and double induction-both of which are important in the modelling of NLP.

Certification and Practitioner Standards

The terms neuro-linguistic programming and NLP are not under the ownership of anyone or any organization. As such, they are not trademarked as intellectual property. There is no central regulatory authority for NLP, and therefore, anybody can describe themselves as an NLP master practitioner or trainer. This has created a situation in which there is a great variation in the standards and training of NLP practitioners, and hence, there is confusion about which practices encompass NLP and which ones do not. There is, therefore, a lack of best practise within the field, which makes it an open field in which everyone develops their own methods and concepts and even brands it as NLP. It is, therefore, essential that you clearly establish who you will be working with and ascertain if your practitioner has a proven track record.

Influencing People Using Neuro-Linguistic Programming

In the above section, we have widely discussed the concept of NLP and given an overview of how the field is like in the 21 st century.

While there are different standards applied by different practitioners, some aspects of the NLP theory remain the same. For example, neuro-linguistic programming can be used effectively to reprogram the human mind in order to achieve success. As a result, you are free to use and apply NLP in all aspects of your life when thinking and communicating in order to achieve different but better outcomes.

We'll use the following scenario as an example:

You must urgently complete a task. However, you simply lack the motivation to do so at this time. You have to do it one way or another.

This may appear to be a critical juncture in life, but there is good news.
You can use NLP techniques to make you feel good about doing the task, and then use the techniques to help you finish it when you feel finished. NLP can help you shift your mindset from one of worry and resentment to one of enjoyment for the task at hand.

Even if you have bad habits, neuro-linguistic programming can be a powerful tool in assisting you to achieve better results once you set out to change them. We outline some NLP secrets below that may be useful for you or the next person in any situation. You will be able to influence not only your own mindset but also the mindsets of others by using these techniques.

Anchoring

Anchoring is an NLP technique that involves attaching anchors to what we see, feel, and hear in order to create emotional states. This means that when you are exposed to a specific stimulus, you form a unique connection between the emotion and the stimulus. If the stimulus occurs again, the emotional state is automatically triggered. Based on this premise, NLP proposes that anchors can be deliberately created to assist people in accessing what is useful to them or achieving a target state.

Returning to the previous example of a person who needs to complete a task but does not feel like it, we can use anchoring to associate the seemingly unpleasant chore with a positive stimulus. When the person in question, for example, decides to eat chocolate because he believes it will improve his concentration and help him achieve more with the job at hand, the next time he needs to do a similar task, he only needs to eat chocolate to feel that his attitude toward the job has significantly improved. Furthermore, because there is an association between chocolate and better attitudes, he will develop a positive attitude every time he eats chocolate.

This is an intriguing concept that builds on Pavlov's ideas. Ivan Pavlov was a Russian physiologist. He conducted research on dogs and their associations with bells. He devised an experiment in which he would ring a bell whenever he was about to feed the dogs.

When they saw the food, they usually started salivating. However, over time, Pavlov discovered that even when the food was not present, the dogs would salivate when the bell rang. Because the ringing of the bell was associated with food, they would salivate automatically in subsequent scenarios, a type of behaviour known as a conditioned response.

Anchoring will thus assist you in associating a positive emotional state with a specific sensation. As a result, you can select a positive sensation and associate it with a gesture. When you activate this anchor while experiencing negative emotions, your feelings will immediately change.

Dissociation

We'll look at a situation to better understand dissociation.

Assume you have a friend. You've fallen in love with her over the course of six months of being around her.

However, your friendship is so strong that whenever you think about approaching her to tell her how you feel, a cold chill runs down your spine. You are afraid that opening up to her will destroy what you think is a good friendship, and you will not be able to recover the friendship if something goes wrong. You, on the other hand, feel compelled to approach her. After all, it's your feelings at stake here. Furthermore, who knows, she might have the same feelings about you. The feelings have become so intense that you feel tense, uncomfortable, and nervous whenever you are near her. Dissociation may be essential in disarming emotions that may otherwise feel automatic to you.

Identify the emotions you want to get rid of before you begin dissociation. In the preceding example, the feelings of tension, discomfort, and nervousness must be removed.

Next, imagine floating out of your body and looking back at yourself and your surroundings from the perspective of another observer. You will notice a significant shift in your emotions at this point.

Dissociate once and watch yourself, then dissociate again and watch yourself watching yourself to get a double dose of good feelings. This is referred to as double dissociation.

This technique is extremely effective at removing negative emotions from a situation.

Reframing of Content

Content reframing is a common yet powerful technique that we are confident you have used at least once in your life.

Here's an example of how content reframing works:

Assume you've just broken up with your boyfriend. You've been dating for three years, which you consider to be a long time. You are depressed, and you are unsure how you will proceed from here because you have invested so much of yourself and time into this relationship. Furthermore, the heartache complicates matters.

You'll notice that in the preceding scenario, you primarily focus on the negative aspects of the breakup. Consider it another way: you are single.

What are the advantages of being single? When you look at your breakup from this angle, you will notice that there is a positive side to it. For example, you are now free to meet new people and, hopefully, find a new life partner. Furthermore, you are not required to answer to anyone about your actions, particularly those that are critical in a relationship. Furthermore, you have learned valuable lessons that you will undoubtedly apply the next time you are in a relationship.

This is an example of content reframing, which is when you give an experience new meaning, resulting in a different experience of the same thing. So, instead of panicking when you're in the thick of things, you can use this technique to shift your focus and have a different experience and make better decisions the next time.

Pacing in the Future

Future pacing entails asking the client to imagine taking action in the future, then observing their reactions to determine whether or not the change process was successful. Before implementing an intervention, the practitioner will assess the client's body language. Following that, he or she will involve the client in a future pacing exercise. If the body remains unchanged, the intervention is deemed ineffective. If, on the other hand, there is a difference in body language, the change was successful. The assumption during visualisation is that the mind cannot distinguish between a visualised scenario and a real one, and thus positive visualisations can be used to set the pace for future reactions because you will already know how to act.

Chapter 4
NLP as a Tool of Persuasion

NLP primarily focuses on assisting people in overcoming negative emotions, bad habits, mental blocks, internal conflict, and other issues. However, there is another branch of NLP that focuses on ethically influencing and persuading others. In this chapter, we will look at hypnosis and persuasion to give you a better understanding of how these tools can be used to your advantage.

Hypnosis

Language patterns are used to persuade others during hypnosis.

Robert Dilts referred to hypnosis as "sleight of mouth," building on the concept of sleight of hand—the magician's ability to make things appear or disappear, despite the fact that it may appear impossible. Milton H. Erickson, a psychiatrist who studied the subconscious mind through hypnosis, was one of the best hypnotists ever known. Erickson became so skilled at his craft that he could communicate with people's subconscious minds without having to hypnotise them. He could hypnotise people at any time and in any place, even during a mundane, everyday conversation, earning the technique the moniker "conversational hypnosis." Over time, hypnosis has evolved into a tool that can not only influence and persuade others, but also help them overcome fear, limiting beliefs, and other obstacles even when they are not consciously aware. When attempting to overcome resistance, the technique can be especially useful. Below, we expound on conversational hypnosis.

Conversational hypnosis does not feature a slick man gazing upon you as you slide into a trance. That may be what Hollywood has taught you. Hypnosis, in reality, happens even in the most unexpected ways and times. For example, did you know that you can go into a trance several times in a day, for instance, when you lose track of time, forget why you came into a room, forget where you placed something or drive to a place and not really remember driving there? It gets even more interesting because even when you talk to yourself, you are technically in a trance. The only difference between this type of hypnosis and conversational hypnosis is that the latter happens during a conversation. So how does it work?

Conscious and Unconscious Control

Humans go into trances when they connect to their subconscious minds. Even when we dream, it is always in a trance, which is the automatic pilot mode of the body. However, this type of hypnosis is not as scary as understanding that someone can simply control your thoughts using speech. It should be a little comforting to understand that the whole of your childhood has been a series of hypnotic episodes as you learned the world and beliefs were instilled into you.

Therefore, as long as you have control over your conscious mind, being hypnotised or hypnotising another may not be such a terrible idea after all.

The real secret behind conversational hypnosis is the same as the basis for traditional hypnosis. In order to hypnotise someone in a conversation, you simply have to prevent information from reaching their conscious minds and encourage it to reach them at a subconscious level. So, how do you do that?

• Through the use of keywords which help to disengage the mind: Interestingly, there are some words which are like keys to the subconscious. A word like imagine acts as a direct command to the subconscious, and the subconscious even begins to act on them even before the conscious mind can filter them. Visualization is key in this type of hypnosis, and that is why such words are used. Let us take an example.

Timothy wants to convince John that taking their business beyond borders will be beneficial for them. However, John does not want the same, and he has reasons that are legitimate. Timothy tries to persuade John for a week, but he does not appear to be budging. His next resort is hypnosis. Timothy says to him: "Imagine if we actualized this dream and expand internationally.

There is a chance that we will be noticed by other multinational companies. Our reputation will grow and our profits will sky-rocket as we shall earn thrice as much as we earn now. This is our gateway to a better life."

There are chances that John has planted a seed of doubt in John's mind, and hence, he will begin to see the possibilities of future success in his head. In the end, John is likely to succumb to the temptation and forget the reasons that initially compelled him to dismiss Timothy in the first place. This only proves that the power of the subconscious mind exceeds that of the conscious one by afar.

• Through the use of vagueness and ambiguity: It is common to hear citizens of different countries complaining that the same ineffective leaders are chosen every election. Now, with the rate of literacy of many individuals in the world, you would think that we are more inclined as a race to make more rational decisions. This makes sense, but what you do not realise is that vagueness and ambiguity is the dirty little secret of most of the world's politicians. In fact, these people are nothing more than a bunch of skilled orators. To prove this claim right, watch out for the next time there is a political campaign in your area.

Take note of the language, specifically, the words that these politicians use to gain the sympathy of voters and garner votes.

You will come to the realisation that their speeches usually lack logic and are full of ambiguous slogans and are ambiguous, serving no real purposes rather than to play with the emotions of the crowd. If a leader intends to use clear, unambiguous speech has a lower probability of winning because often, they cannot whet the emotions of the crowd.

You may wonder how vague and ambiguous language works. It is simple; If someone talks to you in a logical sequence or tells you sentences that make sense, your mind will get to work and begin to decode what the speaker is saying. In the event of doing this, the mind will also be looking for loopholes while trying to decode. If on the other hand, I use ambiguous phrases and words, there is a probability that it will have a tremendous effect on the mind of the masses. While the voter is still trying to decode what the speaker is saying, the speaker is already bombarding them with vaguer information that will override their need to make logical decisions and just voting for them.

For example, a politician may ask the people of a particular city to rise up to the challenge and embrace the coming change. Further, he would tell them that the time is now and that they can do it.

There is a probability that a voter in the crowd will begin to wonder what challenge is being addressed, what change is needed and what time it is when the politician bombards them with the suggestion to vote for him. The subconscious mind processes the suggestion before any information from the conscious is processed.

Creating Rapport

Naturally, many of us tend to fear rats. Imagine getting into a room and finding it full of rats squeaking. Your natural reaction would probably be to shut the door and bolt off or simply get away from that scene. This is the case not because rats will harm you, but more because we as humans are fundamentally different from rats. When we see ourselves as different from a creature, we inherently begin to fear. The same case applies to us within ourselves. We often find that when a person is different from ourselves, we will be afraid of them.

For instance, we are afraid of people we are not familiar with, people of a different religion or we find other cultures and their people strange. This is not a coincidence, as usually, we do not want to cross paths with the unfamiliar. This is the point of creating rapport through techniques like mirroring. These techniques help us make ourselves more familiar and similar to the next person, such that any feelings of fear or awareness created as a result of being different are eliminated.

Rapport involves creating a feeling of confidence and trust.

Creating rapport can be quite easy. However, what is most interesting is that through using this technique, you have the power to get along with almost everyone as it teaches you to relate better with people while creating stronger relationships. These skills are, however, double-edged and they can be used for both good and bad. We believe that as our reader, you will choose to use these techniques for the better.

Mirroring

One effective way of creating rapport is by mirroring. When you mirror, you mimic subtle behaviours when communicating with the next person. Through mirroring, you will feel in connection with one another. Even with little knowledge of each other, you will feel as if you have known each other for eternity. Basically, you will need to mirror someone's movements. Take the example of when you look at yourself in the mirror. When you raise your left eyebrow, the right one \reflects the same in the mirror. This method of creating rapport is so basic and yet so understandable that even chimps use it in their interactions. The same technique applies here, as there are some things you can mirror to gain rapport. They include:

- Gestures
- Posture
- Breathing pattern
- Speech volume and speed
- Tone of voice
- Language

Rapport, in a nutshell, is when your voices and bodies complement each other in a unique way. In fact, communication is often more about the combination of body language and voice tonality than it is about the message being conveyed. As a result, if you learn to control your body language, you will notice a significant improvement in how others perceive you. Mirroring, like any other skill, takes practise, and there are different levels of mirroring that you can achieve.

However, breathing is the most important thing you can mirror because it is an unconscious component of physiology and thus the easiest to notice. You can get an idea of the mirror's breathing pattern by watching her shoulders, especially if she's female. Other areas to consider are the stomach and chest. When attempting to mimic reactions, keep in mind that you should do so in such a way that it appears almost effortless and subconscious. It may appear unnatural at first, but with practise, you will find it easy to mimic. When the skill becomes a part of you, you will do it naturally without even being aware of the efforts you are putting in.

While there are no set rules for mirroring, you can use these techniques to your advantage almost every time. For example, if you notice that a person is primarily audial rather than visual, you can use phrases like "that rings a bell" and "sounds good" to help mirror their senses. If, on the other hand, they are visual, you can speak to them using phrases like "I see" and "It looks good."

You are also better off describing what something sounded like rather than what it looked like if they are audial. Consider an opera as another example. You might want to tell someone that a band's performance was spectacular. However, if a person is more audial than visual, there is no good created describing the facial expressions of the crowd or explaining how the crowds were large. It would, however, be beneficial to tell them of how the violin sounded against the piano and how the voices of the performers sounded. If a person is largely visual, they would appreciate an explanation of how big the crowd was, how the performers looked when they performed, the reactions on the faces in the crowd, and such things. Such use of words helps create a mirroring effect that produces the interest and likeability linked to this technique.

You can match the body language of an individual to create rapport. However, when matching body language, realise that it is not, by any chance, mimicry. As highlighted above, do not mimic every movement as it may seem unnatural, and this may break rapport and destroy any future communication. You should, as such, let the other party take the lead, and you follow and just like you would dance, follow their steps. Take your time to mimic, for example, when someone leans backward, take about 20 to 30 seconds to do the same so that they do not consciously pick upon your actions.

Additionally, it will look natural and not forced. Doing it too soon produces the alternative effect. When matching facial gestures, ensure that you do it well so that it does not look like mockery or feel offensive. For instance, you can smile back at someone that smiles at you, and you can do other things with your face, as long as you are not overdoing it. The subconscious of your partner will pick up these gestures and make him/her think that you two are similar, which creates the feelings of closeness.

When matching voices, you should essentially understand the speed and tone of the individual. This tool is beneficial and effective, especially in the sales sector or if you are limited by phone conversations. A slow and careful pattern of conversation should be mirrored the same way to ensure full effectiveness and vice-versa. To do this effectively, take note of the volume and rhythm used to react.

Getting the rhythm in conversations right can be a bit difficult, but with practice and over time, it begins to come naturally. It may be a good idea to do a bit of voice matching practise with all these resources available for our consumption.

Another tool that you can utilise is pacing and leading. You see in the tools above; we explain how to pace the person you are conversing with. This essentially means that they are leading the conversation. However, for a conversation to be complete, you also have to lead the person your partner to your desired outcome. As such, you have to make them start copying your movement subconsciously as you have been copying theirs. There are several ways you can lead the conversation, but always remember to do it in a positive manner that will be helpful both for you and the next person. Essentially, you have to turn things around, subtly, so that over time, they mirror you. In the end, if, for example, you were making a sale, you will notice that the transaction went rather smoothly.

Chapter 5
Body Language

As we mirror body language, it is equally important to understand just what we are mirroring. Reading body language is important because even before we speak, body language is our first line of communication. Even before you dialogue, eye contact and body language interact to set the pace for the rest of the conversation. That is how we gain first impressions of people, and they gain a first impression of us. Unfortunately, once these assessments have been made, it can be difficult to adjust them to reflect another side of you. It is, therefore, important that you understand how to read body language best. Below, we expound on some aspects of body language:

Finger-Pointing

Picture a scenario where you get into a home, and everything is everywhere. The children are not clean, and there is a general air of dissatisfaction with the current status of the house. The mother searches frantically for the television remote before angrily pointing to her eldest daughter, who is approximately 14 to tell her that the problem in that house us that nobody can return anything to its place.

You are perturbed, but the daughter seems to be just fine, or maybe used to that kind of scenario.

From the scenario above, you can understand the message that the mother is trying to send, clearly. She could not find the remote, and she believed that her eldest daughter was responsible for misplacing it despite the entire house being a mess. However, what is more, evident is the mother is what we would term-a blamer.

Something went wrong in the house, but she was placing all the blame on her daughter. Her language is suggestive, and you would be tempted to wonder where 'around here' refers to and what she means by placing things back in their places. In short, she is trying to pass a message to her daughter that she is irresponsible and careless.

There are some body language signs that also depict weakness.

An example is placating. Placating is by definition, putting the hands at your side with your elbows bent and palms up. It may not seem obvious to you, but when you place your hands this way, you appear to be portraying yourself as a person that is in a position of weakness. As such, you are giving in to the situation, and you have no choice left. If you are a leader in any capacity, this is the kind of gesture you will want to avoid, especially when you need to assert something among peers.

Interestingly, placating can sometimes work to your advantage.

For instance, imagine you have a difficult message to portray. When you use this gesture, it may send a signal of the kind of message you intend to send. Di not, however, overindulge because generally, it elicits the self-pity attitude.

Even though you may expect a different kind of response when such allegations, the daughter remains quiet—as mentioned above, she is probably used to this kind of flare-up. Nonetheless, this is not the kind of reaction you would expect in every other situation. In fact, pointing fingers is looked down upon in many cultures, and once someone takes such an action, it is the kind of body language that will lead to tempers rising and language becoming stronger. This is because pointing fingers sends a message of hostility and is intimidating. You should, as such, be careful how you use your fingers. If you are a parent or teacher, or if you deal with children in any capacity, understand that pointing fingers at them when trying to pass a message may be deleterious. Pointing fingers can be a sign of bullying, and as such, it should not be done to your partner either.

You see, the problem with pointing fingers is that it is the surest way to distract your audience from the message you are trying to pass to them. Even when people do not speak, pointing fingers is usually pretty reflective of what they want to say and elicits feelings of being intimidated and bullied.

Notice that even lawyers use their fingers when speaking.

However, it is very rare to see them using their hands. Instead, they gesticulate-talk with their hands. If they do point, you can be assured that any of the people being pointed at-including witnesses, or even the jury, do not like it. Such behaviour in places such as the courtroom only serve against your favour and may show that you want to push the blame on anyone else but yourself. This is not a courageous act because it may lead to conflict outwardly and is a sign of bullying.

However, it may point to a lack of success or confidence, or isolation at a personal level.

Snapping Fingers

Just like pointing fingers is considered rude, snapping fingers is taken in the same way. Imagine someone trying to get your attention by snapping their fingers at you. It would be a horrible scenario. For instance, in a restaurant, it may be really embarrassing to sit at the same table with a person that snaps his fingers to get the attention of a passing waiter, only to complain about trivial matters. In the end, they will certainly not get better services. Neither will his companions be impressed with his lack of manners and respect for the waiter. The chances are that his friends will avoid dining with him in the future. It would not come as a surprise that such a person is also a fingerpointer and, by extension, a blamer, too. Sometimes, you may feel like these behaviours impress, but honestly, the only person being pleased is you!

Distracting

Distracting is the haphazard use of arms such that the speaker is often switching between different hand positions almost all the time.

While this may seem harmless sometimes, it may have implications on how you are perceived, for instance, by your audience if you are a politician. Switching hand gestures rapidly gives your body a weird angle when viewed. Worse still, it creates confusion. As such, your audience will not understand whether you want to stay where you are, or you are uncertain. When people cannot trust your motives, it is highly unlikely that they will listen to you.

How to Read Body Language — Confident Body Language

Just like there are poor body language signs mentioned above, there are also things that when you do with your hands, you come out as more confident and even calm-which in many cases, adds to your credibility. Below we discuss some of the body language strategies that you may use to your advantage:

Computing

In body language, computing involves placing the elbow of your hand in the other arm then cupping your chin in the free palm. While this is not a technique that is written in many books, it can be useful for you in many scenarios and circumstances. For instance, when coaching, or during a consultation or even when you simply want to lend an ear to the next person. The reason why computing is so powerful is that it creates the impression of a calm and confident person. It may not be easy to adopt such a position when you are in the thick of things, but when used any time possible, the outcomes are likely to be positive.

Apart from depicting calm and confidence, computing shows that you are willing to listen to another person or their point of view. If you want to prove the efficiency of computing, try and see how much more people open up to you when you use it.

Another effective technique that can be used with the hands is known as leveling. If you observe most magistrates, they adopt a stance much like placating, but this time, their palms do not point upwards. Instead, they point downwards. The palms pointing downward conveys the idea of stability. As such, it represents the idea that a speaker is presenting facts as they are and is honest and accurate. If you are trying to reinforce your position while speaking, you can use it alongside other body language techniques such as using the voice to emphasise your point. When you place your hands in this manner, your message is likely to be received positively.

However, be careful and ensure that your words and actions are congruent. You will always notice that when someone speaks, and their hands are not in sync with the message, they risk having themselves misinterpreted.

Talking with the Hands

While snapping and pointing fingers can have negative connotations, it is important to realise that using hands to talk may not be so bad after all. Sometimes, you find that there are individuals that are naturally talented at communicating with their hands and never point fingers or snap. If, however, you have not yet fully grasped the concept when it comes to speaking using the hands, all hope is not lost because you can still train yourself to use your hands effectively.

Have you ever observed that when photographers take pictures, especially those of children, they mostly include the hands?

The reason is simple: the hands add some life, warmth, and comfort to the picture—and they tend to have the same effect in a conversation. The hands are an important tool of communication.

However, if not used well, they appear as a tool for bullying and project hostility. In order to use your hands effectively, just ensure that you avoid pointing and snapping as this is the biggest cause of the feeling that you disrespect someone during a conversation, and balance the use of your hands with the conversation.

The Power in Non-Verbal Communication

In the earlier sections, we mentioned non-verbal communication through techniques such as mirroring and more. But what exactly is the importance of non-verbal communication? Take the case of two people who are speaking and mirroring each other in the process. If one person breaks the pattern, you will notice that both parties falter when there is mismatching behavior. A mismatch sends a message of confusion, insults the person on the receiving end, shocks them, and generally creates negative feelings as it indicates among other things, a lack of interest. If you still do not understand, the scenario above described highlights how potent of a non-verbal tool communication could be. People emotionally respond the most to your non-verbal cues during communication.

How Does This Emotional Reaction Come by?

The intuition usually comes into play when the unconscious mind is picking up and processing non-verbal communication. As such, a shift in your emotions will clearly be depicted to the world outside through non-verbal body and voice signs. This is why when you feel tense, apprehensive, or relaxed, your body will show signs of the same. There are some visible and audible patterns that are observed on the body as a result of the chemical changes that happen within the body. For example, your arms, eyes and leg movements, posture, breathing pattern, pulse on the neck, size of the pupil, and tone of voice, and rate of speech may change. So even when you think you are doing a fabulous job hiding your feelings, someone may notice these physical changes and see through the façade of you hiding what is outwardly obvious. Humans have the ability to pick up on these signs on the other person unconsciously. It occurs as a result of unconscious leakage.

Chapter 6
Influence and Persuasion

Neuro-linguistic programming and persuasion and influence have a strong relationship. To begin, neuro-linguistic programming entails investigating subjective human experience. Essentially, it is the study of how people can create meaning within their minds. Some people believe that neurolinguistic programming entails studying superior thinking. Humans typically generate a sense of meaning both externally and internally. It is also possible to learn more about how people express themselves verbally and how they can be influenced. Language, as an instrument for transmitting internal experiences, can be used to persuade people.

Control by the State

When it comes to influencing and persuading others, the first thing to consider is whether you have a close relationship with the individual. It would be difficult to persuade or influence someone if a personal relationship did not exist. On the other hand, neuro-linguistic programming can be used to develop a personal relationship with someone. Before you can focus on developing a personal relationship, the state control should always come first.

The ability to link various sequences of emotional states at any given time is defined as state control. These techniques can be learned using neuro-linguistic programming. You can also learn more about how to control your state with NLP. If you are able to form a close relationship with someone who was in a bad mood, you should be able to gauge how you felt.

People can feel energised in some situations.

It is also worth noting that if you are not in the right frame of mind, you will find it difficult to form a close relationship with someone, regardless of how well you understand neuro-linguistic programming. When developing a close relationship with someone, you should make sure that your psycho-emotional state corresponds to that of the other party. You will be able to learn a variety of mechanical techniques after studying neuro-linguistic programming, including:

- Using the verbs used by other parties
- Matching the breathing patterns
- Matching the tonalities used by the other party
- Matching their blinking pattern
- Using the posture that they normally use

After learning about neuro-linguistic programming, you can take your own physiology and ensure that it matches the other person's. It is also important to note that a close relationship cannot be formed if you are not physically close to the other person.

The main point to remember is that NLP techniques allow people to speed up the process while also ensuring that their frequency can align with that of the other person in a short period of time.

Classical neuro-linguistic programming allows you to easily assume the character of the other party and persuade and influence them. It is also possible to completely replicate the individual. Pacing is a term used to describe such an occurrence. Pacing entails imitating someone or talking about things that may or may not be true depending on the situation.

You may want to form a close relationship with someone who is in a bad mood but are unsure how to go about it. According to various professionals, you may want to form a bond with someone who is in a bad mood, but you do not want to be in the same bad mood as them. Such consideration arises from the fact that you must be in the same state as the person with whom you wish to establish contact. Some of the phenomena that appear in plat include the presence of mirror neurons, which can assist you in forming the desired connection with the other party.

It is also possible to alter someone's current state. When approaching someone, you may have several options, including interrupting them, and you must first observe the surroundings. Most people may also lack the courage to speak up in front of others. The other instance entails making certain that you can match the other person's state. They can easily change the state of the other individual by changing their state to their own.

When you approach someone and exhibit high energy levels, there may be a significant difference in the frequency of the two parties, and you may be unable to relate. For example, your energy levels may be higher than the target individual's, implying that your states cannot align. Furthermore, some states are not easily interrupted. You will still relate if you form a connection with someone and your frequencies do not align.

How to Succeed in a Job Interview

You should be persuasive when attending a job interview. You should also think about how you can persuade the interviewer. In such a case, you should make certain that you can establish a close relationship with the interviewer.

It is beneficial to ask a variety of questions in order to learn more about the other person. During the phone interview, you should also make sure that you have highlighted the main reason why you are a good fit for the job. Because the interviewer has the authority to decide whether or not you will be hired, you are expected to cooperate. It is also difficult to define the ideal employee because everyone has different values and characteristics.

During an interview, use your state, language, mirror neurons, and intention to ensure that you have the interviewer's attention. You can interact with them on a specific level. While the interviewer is discussing the ideal employee, you should go over your resume to see if you have the qualities that the interviewer is looking for. It is also possible to determine whether or not you are the ideal employee. Always pay attention to the important details.

Establish your credibility: The interview is a process in which the interviewer attempts to identify the most trustworthy candidate who can do the job. As a result, you should demonstrate to them that you are the best candidate for the job.

You can accomplish this by establishing a relationship or demonstrating your expertise. Include words and answers that reflect trends in your field in the expertise section. To start a relationship, demonstrate that you share common interests and are aware of current events. You can also demonstrate expertise by emphasising your previous accomplishments as well as what you hope to achieve in the future. You can ask them questions about their experiences in order to create an interactive session.

"What's in it for me?" asks the dreaded question. People are often afraid to ask what a job offers simply because they are the ones looking. Don't just sell your advantages; ask them what they can offer you as well. This demonstrates to them that you value yourself and are willing to accept only the best.

Paint a picture: If you recall what we said about conversational hypnosis in the preceding sections, you should have no trouble painting a picture. Visualize your examples so that they stick in the interviewer's mind. Giving an analogy or metaphor may be more beneficial than you realise. Don't forget to include some heart, as displaying your true self can only benefit you.

Chapter 7
Manipulation

Everyone has used manipulation at some point in their lives to achieve something—and that's fine because it's almost always a matter of survival. However, doing so at the expense of others is wrong and deceptive. This chapter delves into manipulation by explaining what it is, the different types of manipulation, the tactics used during manipulation, what to do if you suspect you are being manipulated, and much more! Continue reading to find out what you need to know to deal with the problem.

What Exactly Is Manipulation?

Manipulation is the indirect interference in another person's decision-making without their consent. It is a type of social influence in which underhanded, indirect toe deceptive tactics are used to change the perceptions and behaviours of others. A manipulator's motivating actions vary and can be especially devious and exploitative. However, it is critical to recognise that social influence does not always have to be negative. For example, family, friends, or even lawyers can sometimes try to persuade someone to change their minds, and usually it is for their own good, such as encouraging a change in behaviour that may land them in legal trouble. In fact, social influence is generally regarded as harmless as long as it respects the person being influenced's right to reject or accept it. In the case of manipulation, on the other hand, the manipulator's motivations are shady, making it the polar opposite of positive social influence.

Manipulation of the Mind

The goal of psychological manipulation is to get the victim to act impulsively, automatically, and reflexively. Typically, the manipulative person acts beyond their competence to influence the behaviour of the other person in accordance with their self-serving wishes and goals. This type of manipulation occurs when one person attempts to seize the right to rule over the life of another person despite the fact that they do not have the legal authority to do so.

When it comes to successful manipulation, various theories have been proposed. They are as follows:

Braiker's Hypothesis

Harriet B. Braiker identified the various ways in which a manipulator can control the victim, which include:

1. Reinforcement that is sporadic. This occurs, for example, in the case of gambling. In most cases, the gambler loses money overall but occasionally wins. However, this type of control can create an environment of doubt and fear, and these circumstances can sometimes encourage the victim to persist.

2. Providing positive reinforcement. Positive reinforcement includes the use of superficial charm, praise, superficial sympathy, forced laughter or smiling, and public recognition.

3. Reverse reinforcement. Negative reinforcement entails taking a person out of a negative situation.

4. Sanctions. Silent treatment, yelling and nagging, playing the victim, sulking and crying, emotional blackmail, guilt trip, threats, and intimidation are all forms of punishment.

5. One-trial traumatic learning: Explosive anger, verbal abuse, displays of dominance or superiority, and other one-time behavioural techniques that can train the victim to avoid confronting, contradicting, or upsetting the manipulator are examples of traumatic one-trial learning.

Simon's Hypothesis

According to George K. Simon, successful manipulation entails the manipulator concealing their intentions and behaviours while remaining friendly, understanding the psychological vulnerability of the victim so that they know which tactics are most likely to be effective, and being ruthless when causing harm to the victim. Manipulation is accomplished through both covert and aggressive means. In this case, the following strategies were employed:

1. Lying by omission: Lying by omission is the deliberate withholding of a significant truth from a person. This is a common tactic used by those who use propaganda.

2. Lying by commission: The most common type of lying that you are used to is lying by commission. It can be difficult to tell if someone has simply lied to you at times, but it becomes clear over time. This can happen when it is too late. Understanding that personality types such as narcissists and psychopaths are more prone to lying than other personality types is one good way to ensure or at least reduce your chances of being lied to. Those in the dark triad discussed above are often experts at not only lying but also cheating, and they do it frequently and in the most subtle of ways.

3. Minimization: A manipulator will frequently rationalise a lie by explaining why he did it and then deny it in a way that absolves him/her of responsibility. They usually do this by attempting to persuade people that their behaviour is not as harmful or dangerous as others claim. These are the people who will frequently tell you that

an insult was merely a joke and other such nonsense. This may be a hurtful remark, but it is frequently used as a means to an end. They should not be able to persuade you that it was not an unintentional remark on their part.

4. Rationalization: We briefly mentioned rationalisation above. Making an excuse for the manipulator's behaviour is referred to as rationalisation. This excuse is used to make the person being manipulated believe that the action was justified.

5. Selective attention: Selective attention and selective inattention are closely related. The manipulator willfully ignores what the person they are attempting to manipulate says. When you hear statements like, "I don't want to listen to you right now," it's possible that a manipulation technique is taking root.

6. Diversion: A diverting road is one that takes a different path than the 'main' road. This is a tactic used by the manipulator that involves steering the conversation to a different topic and not providing a direct answer when necessary.

7. Evasion: Diversion is required for evasion. What distinguishes this tactic is the use of weasel words and giving vague, irrelevant, rambling responses rather than a diversion from the main topic.

8. Guilt-tripping: Many manipulators use guilt-tripping as a unique yet powerful tool. The manipulator suggests to the victim that they have it easy, are too selfish, and do not care enough about them, which keeps the other party in a state of submission, self-doubt, and anxiety. The manipulator has complete control over the victim while in this position.

9. Covert intimidation: This technique involves using veiled threats to put the victim on the defensive.
    Threats that are veiled are subtle, implied, and sometimes indirect.

10. Shaming: In this case, the manipulator employs sarcasm and other techniques to humiliate the victim. When the victim believes they are unworthy, they defer to the manipulator. Shaming tactics vary in nature and can sometimes take the most subtle forms, such as a sneer or a fierce look, an unpleasant voice tone, or a rhetorical comment. When this happens, the victims are usually so embarrassed that they are unable to confront or vilify the manipulator. Shaming makes the

victim feel insufficient.

11. Pretending to be a victim: Most manipulators pretend to be victims in order to gain sympathy and compassion. This is typically done in order to obtain something from another person. They prey on conscientious and caring people, who would normally be unable to bear the sight of another person in pain. They arouse sympathy in order to facilitate cooperation.

12. Victim vilification: When the victim stands up for themselves, the manipulator sometimes accuses them of being abusive. This is another strategy used by manipulators that is very effective because it masks the manipulator's aggressive intent while putting the person being manipulated on the defensive. In such a situation, it is easy to overlook the true victim, making this tactic even more effective.

13. Blame projection: A manipulator will frequently use another person as a scapegoat when projecting blame.
They accomplish this by projecting their thoughts onto the targeted victim, making them believe they have done something wrong. After duping them into believing their lies, victims frequently blame the victim for believing in what were clearly lies. At this point, the victim may wonder if they forced the manipulator to be deceptive; all lame at this point is directed at the victim, making them feel guilty for making any good choices or acting well. In this case, the victim may become confused because the manipulator will continue to lie about lying and remanipulate what has already been manipulated.
This tactic is frequently used as a control tool as well. As a result, the manipulators will accuse the victim of deserving harsh treatment and then label them as crazy, abusive, and other things that they are not, especially when evidence is presented against the manipulator.

14. Seduction: The manipulator may use flattery, charm, praise, and overt support of others to lower their defences and possibly offer their loyalty to the manipulator. In such cases, manipulators may offer their assistance so that the unsuspecting victim gives their loyalty and ends up in a position where they are being manipulated and controlled.

15. Acting as a servant: Manipulators will sometimes 'suck up' in order to conceal their self-serving agendas. They pose as servants and pretend to be obedient while they wait for the perfect opportunity to carry out their plans. This is especially true when an authority figure is involved.

16. Pretending to be confused: Manipulators will go to any length to deal with their victims. For example, it is not uncommon for the manipulator to act as if they do not completely understand their victim. In such cases, they will pretend that they do not understand what the victim is saying or that they are perplexed about something that has just been brought to their attention. As a result, the victim is confused by the manipulator, and they begin to doubt their own perception accuracy. If you've ever found yourself highlighting key elements that someone else highlighted in order to judge yourself and your judgement, you've most likely been a victim of a manipulator's confusion tactics. Manipulators may even use cohorts to advance their stories.

17. Pretending to be confused: Manipulators will go to any length to deal with their victims. For example, it is not uncommon for the manipulator to act as if they do not completely understand their victim. In such cases, they will pretend that they do not understand what the victim is saying or that they are perplexed about something that has just been brought to their attention. As a result, the victim is confused by the manipulator, and they begin to doubt their own perception accuracy. If you've ever found yourself highlighting key elements that someone else highlighted in order to judge yourself and your judgement, you've most likely been a victim of a manipulator's confusion tactics. Manipulators may even use cohorts to advance their stories.

18. Using anger: The manipulator may use his anger to elicit an emotional response from you as the victim.

They use emotional intensity and, at times, rage to shock the victim into submission. What makes this tactic evil is that, in most cases, the manipulator is not even angry and is simply acting. As a result, they will demand what they want and, when denied, will put on a 'angry show.' This type of anger is usually controlled and used as a deterrent to avoid confrontation. They may use it to avoid being truthful and to conceal any additional intentions they may have toward the victim.

Within this tactic, you will find the manipulator threatening to call the cops, reporting false abuse, or using other techniques to force or scare the victim into submission. Also, when other tactics fail, they usually use blackmail and other forms of controlled anger to force submission. In this way, they avoid any suspicions or further inquiries that could lead to the revelation of the manipulator's true intent. The victim is made to focus on the manipulator's rage rather than facts, allowing them to be manipulated before they realise it.

19. Using the bandwagon effect: The bandwagon effect is a manifestation of mob mentality. This occurs when someone does something simply because others have done it before them. Peer pressure, for example, is a type of bandwagon effect because most teenagers find themselves doing what other teenagers are doing. However, in this case, the manipulator dupes his victim into doing something simply because others have done it. When you hear phrases like "other people your age," "people like you," "you are the odd one out," and others, it is likely that a form of manipulation is at work.

Manipulative People's Characteristics

Manipulators have mastered the art of deception, as we have discovered. They may appear respectable, but this is usually just a ruse to fool the rest of the world into believing them before they reveal their true colours to the victims. Remember that a manipulative person is not genuinely interested in you, because to them, you are just a pawn in the game, a means to an end. They frequently have a variety of methods for achieving their objectives and have a keen eye for detail. Manipulators can be identified from a distance before they enter your mind and make you feel confused and insane. To help protect you from the tentacles of the manipulator, we've highlighted some of their characteristics below:

• They believe that their approach to a problem is the only one available. Furthermore, they have no insight into the scenarios they create when interacting with others when their needs are not met. They are self-centered, and only their own needs are important to them. Every relationship or situation they find themselves in has to be about them and no one else, or what those other people think or feel. These people never question themselves, and they always blame someone else. If you find yourself in the company of someone whose best bet is to make you feel as if you can never get anything right, you are most likely in the company of a manipulator, and it may be time to tread lightly, taking care not to become entangled in their web of lies.

• You may understand the word boundary and its implications in how you interact with others, but the manipulator does not or chooses not to. As a result, they pursue their goals with zeal, without regard for who they hurt along the way, and with little regard for everyone else. These people will frequently overstep their emotional, physical, psychological, and physical boundaries in your presence and will not be bothered. They are unconcerned about your personal identity or your personal space. They, like parasites, will degrade, exhaust, and weaken you in order to breach your boundaries and defences. If you notice such disregard for boundaries in someone you frequently interact with, it could be a manipulator softening you up as prey for their own self-serving reasons.

• Manipulators prey on your emotions, conscientiousness, and sensibilities. If you believe that manipulators lack emotional intelligence, you may be mistaken. In fact, they can quickly identify your emotional capabilities and know which ones to investigate. They frequently lead you into a relationship because they recognise your positive qualities, such as kindness and caring. If you are the type who is always willing to assist, be on the lookout for a manipulator. They frequently begin by appealing to your kindness by praising you for being such a nice and kind person, and they may be generally nice to you. However, you will notice that the number of compliments has decreased significantly over time. If you find yourself in this situation, understand that you are only being used to serve a person who doesn't care if you are okay or not. What matters most to them is what you have to offer them and nothing else.

• Manipulators are also expert triangulators. They create dynamics and scenarios in which people become entangled in a web of jealousy, competition, and, as a result, disharmony. Take note of how the people around you speak about other people. You might notice that one person has distinct communication patterns. If you catch someone talking about other people behind your back while you're around, there's a good chance they'll do the same to others. If their words in relation to others are mean and harsh, there is a chance that you will be a victim of the same circumstances in the presence of other people. Similarly, there is a chance that you are dealing with a master manipulator who is only playing his/her cards to put you all in a position where he/she has complete control.

• Have you ever met someone who seemed intent on misinterpreting you? You may have just been graced by the mighty presence of a manipulator. In such a case, stop attempting to explain yourself to such a person because you will not only waste your energy, but you will also be emotionally drained. This is one way the manipulator may trick you into staying and fulfilling their selfish needs. Refuse to make it your mission to make them understand or even like you because manipulators are rarely genuinely interested in you as a person.

• You may notice that a person's words do not always correspond to their actions. We recommend that you focus on a person's actions to determine whether or not their words are true. What you say and what you do can be diametrically opposed. When you stop making excuses for people when passing judgement, you will be able to see right through their lies and manipulation.

• Manipulators are also known to appear to be skilled when, in fact, they are only pretending to be. If you find yourself in a situation where someone appears to be acting good, it is likely that they are just hiding behind a mask, and you should tread carefully if you become involved with them. Manipulators may know how to conceal their intentions, but the veil that conceals their deception may be visible for a brief moment. If you are fortunate enough to have read this information, you may have just saved yourself from an encounter with a manipulator.

To protect yourself from a manipulator, you may need to challenge yourself to learn more about yourself. As a result, you should conduct regular self-evaluations. While doing so, you should consider who you are and what you believe. You change over time and as you get older, but the core of your character never changes. Assess yourself to determine the extent of the shift in your attitudes and beliefs. When you understand yourself, you can thwart any attempts by the manipulator to breach your defences, as opposed to those who do not understand what they believe in. As a result, manipulating your thoughts becomes more difficult.

Who are the Manipulators' Favorite Victims?

Manipulators typically target people with vulnerabilities because they see them as buttons that can be pushed to their advantage. For example, if you are always eager to please, addicted to earning approval and acceptance from others, are not assertive and generally cannot say no to any sort of advances even when they are clearly playing to your disadvantage, and lack a strong sense of identity, you may be a candidate for the manipulator.

Manipulators will also take advantage of the following flaws:

• Innocence. You are a good person who does not want to believe that anyone in the world can be devious, cunning, or even ruthless for no reason. Even when confronted with a manipulator, you refuse to believe that they are victimising you. You can't believe, after all these years, that people who are manipulative exist and can get away with it. You may be going through a naive phase, but you will soon realise that this is just another vulnerability that the manipulator sees and exploits.

• Excessive conscientiousness. If you are overly conscientious, it means you are too willing to give the manipulator the benefit of the doubt. You are willing to look at the world from a different angle—their angle. The worst part about such a scenario is that, at the end of the day, you will be held responsible, despite your best efforts to see things differently.

• Excessive intellectualization. You believe in logic, so you make an effort to comprehend the manipulator. You believe he/she has a reason for acting the way he/she does, and you are correct. The only difference is that these reasons are unjustifiable, and you will end up losing.

• Lack of self-assurance. Because they have highly developed social skills, master manipulators can detect self-doubt from a long distance. When they identify you as a target, they realise it will be easy for you to go on the defensive, so they will attack.

• Emotional reliance. When you lack confidence in yourself, your personality is likely to be dependent and submissive, which is exactly what a manipulator requires to get their way with you. You are more likely to be manipulated and even exploited in this state. They recognise that you, as an emotionally dependent individual, require love and are thus gullible enough to agree to things you should not.

It is unfortunate that manipulators can prey on vulnerable groups such as the elderly, because the elderly are more likely to become fatigued as their cognitive abilities deteriorate. When they are listening to a sales pitch, for example, they will be unable to consider the possibility of being a conman. As a result, they are more likely to succumb and even give their money to a manipulator. Even if you are too honest, fair, and even empathetic, you are vulnerable to manipulative tactics. People who make rash decisions and are generally impulsive are more likely to become entangled in a manipulator's web of lies because they will make a decision most of the time without considering the full range of possible consequences. If you are lonely, it is also important to be on the lookout because you may be hungry for human contact at this time, which the manipulator may be aware of and use to their advantage. Manipulators may be drawn to negative traits such as greed because they understand how to entice the victim to act immorally.

The Manipulator's Motives

When dealing with manipulators, it is common to wonder what they gain from such experiences. Manipulation is essentially a game of power, and some of the manipulator's motivations are listed below. The list is not exhaustive, but it is what motivates them.

• Advancement of their own purpose and personal gain: This usually comes at the expense of others, and they don't care how far they have to go to achieve their goals. A manipulator, unlike any other person, will not accept no for an answer, and they will go to any length to ensure their objectives are met. They believe that the end justifies the means. A manipulator has thus learned to be ruthless over time, and they only care about themselves.

• They have a strong desire to feel powerful. Normally, they are deficient on the inside. This means they are not as powerful as they portray themselves to be. After their initial resistance is broken, they gain satisfaction from manipulating others and wielding power as a result of their state. As a result, their relationships are a series of situations in which they must edify themselves while underplaying the victims' power.

They are also prone to having low self-esteem. The ability to wield power through manipulation allows them to feel as if they have improved their self-esteem. They feel better about themselves when they manipulate others and believe you will see them as bigger than they are. Remember that a manipulator has power only when you give it to them, so you should always be on the lookout so that no one pushes you around without your permission.

• They want to be in charge. Manipulative people dislike the idea that someone else can take control. They are always striving to be ahead of everyone else, despite the fact that they lack power. As a result, they seize control through deception and manipulation. This sense of self-control validates them, and they believe that they are better off as a result.
Manipulation enables them to achieve control as both a desire and a necessity.

• They want to put an end to monotony. Sometimes life is just a series of mundane activities, and there isn't much we can do about it. People usually sit out a boring phase of their lives and wait for something exciting to happen. Manipulators, on the other hand, are not like that. For them, the question is, "Why be bored when you can spice up your own life?" If chaos erupts unexpectedly in a place of relative peace and you suspect it is the result of manipulation, consider what a manipulator would do when bored. Boredom with their surroundings is not an option for manipulators. Sometimes their manipulation is simply a means of alleviating boredom. In fact, they do not believe they are causing you harm. For them, it's all part of a little game.

• They have a hidden agenda. Covert agendas are agendas that are hidden. The manipulator, you see, will manipulate you in order to achieve a goal that they do not want you to know about. For example, a criminal plot in which you serve as a pawn. In the case of financial manipulation, the manipulator would approach the elderly or other unsuspecting wealthy individuals. They would specifically target them for one reason: to seize their financial assets, and their actions, while incomprehensible to the untrained eye, would be intended to achieve this hidden agenda. • Sometimes, they manipulate unconsciously. While manipulators are often masters of deception, some of them are not doing it for the sake of pleasure or power. They do it because they are unaware of the underlying emotions and have a fear of commitment, most likely as a result of having to deal with deception from others in their early lives. When they manipulate unconsciously, they do so to invalidate their own emotions.

How Do You Know If You've Been Duped by a Psychological Manipulator?

I mentioned earlier in the chapter how we've all probably manipulated someone else. This type of manipulation has mostly come to us subconsciously; however, there are people who enjoy malicious manipulation. Such manipulators are not only skilled, but they have also done their homework. They know not only what to do but also which buttons to push, and it can be very easy for them to get into your nerves and get whatever they want out of you before you can blink and realise what is going on. This is why it is critical for you to be able to see through an emotionally manipulative person's intentions and behaviour. If you are unable to distinguish one manipulator from another, you may suffer from emotional trauma. We've highlighted some of the ways you can tell if you're being manipulated psychologically below:

• You are made to feel responsible for the transgressions of others.
Emotional manipulators have mastered the art of shifting blame to others. If you have that one person around you who knows how to find complicated ways to blame you, you may be a victim of manipulation. For example, you could have left them with your cat for the weekend with specific instructions on what the feline should eat. The feline consumes what you have prescribed, but the manipulator adds something to the cat's food that you have not recommended, and the cat becomes ill. When you inquire, the manipulator will most likely claim that you did not state that the acat should not eat anything else and that you did not call to ensure that the cat only ate what you left. If you ever find yourself in this situation, it is very likely that the person you are dealing with is manipulating you. At the end of the day, you'll find yourself apologising for something you didn't do, which lowers your self-esteem and wears out your self-worth over time. • They always play the victim. In the example above, you can see that the person is blaming someone else and, in essence, playing the victim. If a person acts as if they are not responsible for a mess and blames others, you should understand that the person is not only unwilling to accept responsibility, but also a master manipulator who understands well that they can get people to do their bidding using such techniques.

• They tell lies about insignificant matters. You may notice that someone lies a lot, even when it is completely unnecessary.

When this happens, you should recognise the person as a manipulator because they have grown accustomed to weaving a web of lies in which even minor details are twisted.

These minor lies usually serve no purpose and consume so much of the manipulator's time that they are unable, to tell the truth even when it is not necessary to lie.

• Their actions and words are as indistinguishable as water and paraffin. When paraffin is added to water, it separates into a heterogeneous mixture, with the water sinking to the bottom and the paraffin floating on top. It is also widely accepted that actions speak louder than words. You see, a manipulator's actions and words are distinct. They are masters of language, frequently using it to persuade their unsuspecting victims so that they can achieve their goals. They will, however, never keep their end of the bargain. Instead, they will use flattering words to lull you into a false sense of security, but they will never keep their word. They will break almost every single promise they make. If this has ever happened to you, you may be dealing with a manipulator, and you must understand that these things happen because they never intended to keep their promises in the first place. If there were a pain Olympics, the manipulators would easily win every time. Manipulators enjoy eliciting sympathy and will do so at any opportunity. What better time to do so than when they hear someone describe a seemingly painful ordeal or struggle? They will string your situation or struggle into nothing before coming up with a more outrageous, well-crafted wilder, and more sympathetic version of events involving them. They hope that by doing so, they will be able to win the day and gain your sympathy. They are skilled at feigning mutual trust. They may be cunning, but they understand that in order to deceive you, they must first gain your trust.

So, what do they decide? They decide to create a false sense of trust between the two of you. These tools, when combined with sympathy, will work wonders to make them a star in your eyes. How do they appear to have mutual trust? They accomplish this by demonstrating to you how much they trust and value you in a unique way. For example, if you are in a relationship with a manipulator, they may regard you as their most trusted confidant. If you're a friend, they might try to persuade you that you're their closest and best friend.

They will literally make you appear to be the best thing that has ever happened to them. Don't be duped. Manipulators understand that in order to earn your trust and get you to reciprocate, they must act as if you are the centre of their universe. You will then feel obligated to return the trust because you will have no reason not to. It is a natural human instinct to want to trust others, and when others show their trust in us, we are likely to feel guilty if we do not reciprocate. The catch-22 with the manipulator's false trust is that the intimacy they share with their victims is always unquestionably fake. They share false information and experiences with you because they do not want to provide you with ammunition to bring them down. When dealing with people, be cautious because it can be difficult to tell whether what you are handed is a tool for manipulation or not.

• They put you in a position where you believe they are negotiating. The most common way they do this is by asking a question that leads you to believe you reached a compromise when in fact you did not. For example, if they want $200 from you, they will not ask for it directly. They will come to you hoping to get up to $500 and will actually ask for more. If you say you don't have $500, they soften their tone and say, "Well, the situation is dire; even $2000 will suffice."

As a normal person, it would be easier to give in to this demand and believe you have reached an agreement. The real truth, however, is that you were duped, and the dupe knew exactly how to get the $200 out of your pockets.

All in all, keep in mind that emotional manipulation is real, and it can be difficult to detect it at times. However, with the tips we've given you in the preceding section, there's a chance you'll be able to sniff out a potential manipulator.

Also, remember that you are deserving, that your judgement is almost always correct, and that no one should ever put you in a position where you question your own sanity or judgement. Nobody should tell you what to do, and no one should impose something that is not true on you while you are watching them, even if they are manipulative.

Manipulators are aware that they are manipulating others. Is There a Scientific Basis for This Behavior?

We've talked a lot about determining if you're a victim of a manipulator and how to spot one in the previous segments. While this is not necessarily a bad thing, few people stop to consider what happened to these people and what makes them the way they are. In order to better understand the manipulator, we will discuss whether these people are aware that they are manipulating others and what causes them to be so. This is not to say that you should try to understand, validate, or condone the manipulator in your life; rather, it is a call to understand them and what motivates their nefarious motives.

The answer to whether manipulators are usually aware of manipulation is yes. Manipulators eventually realise that their communication style differs from that of others. What happens is that these people have often learned to ask for things in the wrong way, and they have come to realise that the way they handle things may be different, if not incorrect. However, they are content with the current state of affairs. Manipulators can be compared to children who never grew up. They project an image of invincibility and display well-thought-out schemes and bold deception, emitting an aura of power that many of us have come to fear.

Many people are unaware that manipulators are diametrically opposed to the objects they seek to manipulate. In fact, these people are frequently terrified. They are afraid of the person they are manipulating, which is why they work so hard to make you feel smaller than they are. Furthermore, these people are vulnerable and may be terrified on the inside. What they see on the outside is not what they are feeling on the inside. However, by removing reality as it is, they feel safe on the inside. Everything they do is to avoid confrontation, to feel in control, and to achieve their goals as best they can. Most manipulators are children on the inside, and they did not grow out of the typical manipulative phase that all children go through. Their development came to a halt when it was disrupted, for example, by a lack of parental presence, which is required for a child to grow into an exemplary adult. They then began to study the people around them and discovered that certain words are used and what effects these words have. They want the same things that everyone else wants, but they go about it in the wrong way.

Borderline Personality Disorder and Manipulation

The dark triad is one group that is particularly linked to the vice of manipulation. It goes without saying that those in the dark triad are mostly master manipulators. However, other personality disorders, such as borderline personality disorder, can appear manipulative. One question you may have is whether they are aware that they are being manipulative. In this section, we will look at borderline personality disorder to see if they are manipulative in nature.

A borderline personality disorder affects about 2% of the population and is characterised by intense and unstable interpersonal relationships as well as poorly regulated emotions. People with this personality also have poor emotion regulation, self-destructive impulses, and an unstable self-image.

When you're around them, you'll always be walking on eggshells because their emotions will undergo complete transformations in short periods of time, and they frequently have trouble controlling themselves, resulting in unwanted scenarios in which they feel a lack of self-worth while the onlooker is left perplexed. Typically, the person with the personality disorder feels the need to express their agitation in some way, which may not be in the most pleasant way. This high level of discomfort drives them to actions that can be self-mutilating, and they sometimes engage in self-destructive behaviours such as reckless sex, overspending, binge eating, and substance abuse. People suffering from borderline personality disorder may commit suicide in the worst-case scenario.

If you've ever lived with or even fallen in love with someone who has borderline personality disorder, you know that they can be some of the most difficult people to love. They are difficult to love not because they are bad people, but because they approach situations differently. For example, they are drama queens who can conjure up chaotic situations from the most mundane of circumstances. Many readers will agree with the statements made above, but what many people do not realise is that people with borderline personality disorder are different from other people because they experience the mental effects of rage, anxiety, and emptiness more intensely than people who do not have the disorder. The intensity of their pain is what distinguishes them from other people with personality disorders. Most people who experience abandonment are victims of abusive or sadistic environments. A person with bipolar disorder has unique needs, and they frequently find themselves trapped in a world that makes it difficult for them to function because it is often filled with indifferent or insensitive people who don't care what the next person is doing.

While working in this indifferent world may be easy, even enjoyable for a normal person, it is not the case for someone suffering from a borderline personality disorder. They do not find strength in the challenges posed by a world that can be hostile, even to the healthy ego. It can be difficult, given that having a personality disorder means you don't have a healthy ego to fall back on in times of trouble. While it may appear impossible and even bizarre, people with borderline personality disorder can only thrive on consistent support, affection, and love, and if this is not provided, they begin to lash out in fear of feelings of abandonment that may arise as a result of a situation. Furthermore, labelling them as manipulative makes it even more difficult to survive because it contributes to a further misunderstanding of borderline personality disorder. Their feelings of insecurity and instability are the result of an illness caused by neurological imbalances and the environment in which they live. This disorder is distinguished by the fact that it manifests so strongly in relationships, in contrast to other conditions that people may have.

Consider schizophrenia: a schizophrenic person can coexist peacefully with others, is unlikely to cause problems for those with whom they interact, and may not stand out in any way from other people. A person with borderline personality disorder, on the other hand, must only interact with people, and even one interaction can be fatal.

BPD is frequently misdiagnosed as bipolar disorder, which is understandable given that both disorders involve mood changes. Mood changes in bipolar patients, on the other hand, are caused by patterns of sleep disruption and high levels of energy. In contrast, BPD is triggered by an incident. Unlike bipolar disorder, which has typical highs and lows, borderline personality disorder has highs and lows that can change in less than an hour.

This personality disorder is also likely to coexist with other mental illnesses such as depression. Depression is so common in people with borderline personality disorder that up to 80% of those with BPD suffer from it. Anxiety affects 90 percent of people with BPD, bulimia affects 26 percent, PTSD affects another 26 percent, and bipolar disorder affects 10 percent.

It is important to recognise that these characters' actions can have an impact on us, but it would be considerate to consider how it feels to be in their shoes. Because of their poor social skills and inappropriate behaviour, borderline personality disorder patients are difficult to care about. It is also difficult to show compassion because the disorder frequently results in a vicious cycle in which one person requires more love than they would if they were normally functional.

Furthermore, there is a general lack of knowledge and awareness, which leads to stigma. There are myths surrounding borderline personality disorder, which does not help matters. As a result, people with this personality disorder are often misunderstood and stereotyped as manipulative. People suffering from BPD are prone to unintentional and dysfunctional manipulation. However, there is still a stigma surrounding those with this disorder, making them appear as if they intentionally manipulate other people and are generally bad. The name of this disorder, we believe, contributes to the misconceptions surrounding it. If you conduct a Google search for the term "borderline," the results may be perplexing to you or others. There may be mention of other borderline issues, such as borderline schizophrenia, which has nothing to do with schizophrenia. Such ambiguity and lack of clarity do nothing to help alleviate the disorder's misconceptions. Another reason for the stigmatisation of people with BPD is that the disorder manifests primarily in the context of relationships. If you've ever been in a relationship with someone who has BPD, you know how intense, volatile, and demanding these relationships can be. They also have a fear of abandonment, which can have a negative impact on you as the recipient of all their energy. While people are open about their struggles with other mental illnesses and personality disorders, few people talk about borderline personality disorder as much as they should, despite the fact that it is more common than other personality disorders such as bipolar. Some therapists believe that borderline personality disorder is incurable in severe cases. As a result, some refuse to accept patients who have been diagnosed with BPD.

There is, however, a light at the end of the tunnel for these patients, as Marsha Linehan, a psychologist and BPD patient herself, discovered an effective, revolutionary cognitivebehavioral treatment called dialectical behaviour therapy in the 1970s. This therapy emphasises a strong and equal relationship between the patient and the therapist. In this type of therapy, the therapists use a philosophical exercise in which they discuss two opposing viewpoints with the patient until they reach a balance in the extremes. In this way, the patient's feelings and actions are acknowledged as understandable, and they are encouraged to change to more adaptable, healthier, and non-disruptive approaches. While there is no FDA-approved medication treatment for BPD, the symptoms are usually treated with medication that targets co-occurring disorders. Antidepressants, anti-anxiety medications, and mood stabilisers can help reduce the mood swings experienced by people with this personality disorder.

What you need to understand is that people with borderline personality disorder may appear to be manipulative, but their actions are usually far from manipulative.

Borderline personality disorder causes people to act impulsively as a result of intense pain, and the resulting behaviours are not as deliberate as those of the dark triad. As a result, they can't be considered truly manipulative. In fact, manipulation was removed as a defining feature of borderline personality disorder in psychology.

How to Handle Manipulation

Before we go any further into the topic of manipulation, it's important to remember that the first rule of dealing with manipulative people is to make sure you're safe. If your relationship with a manipulator makes you feel unsafe, you must devise a plan to ensure your safety. This can include moving out of your home permanently and staying away for an indefinite period of time. Other steps you can take to deal with a manipulator outside of the home, such as the workplace, are discussed below:

• Ignore, ignore, and then some. Manipulators use frustration and confusion as tools of their trade. If you find yourself in a confrontation with a manipulator, it is unwise to try to correct them. Whatever they do, act as if you are completely unaware of it. When manipulators attack, they do so in order to learn what emotionally triggers you. When you decide to correct them, you are entering a trap, and they know exactly how to frustrate you and use your triggers to influence how you will act.

• Use their own strategies to your advantage. Giving the manipulator a taste of their own medicine is what this entails. You must have realised by now that manipulators employ a variety of tactics against you. They are, however, equally human and have the same perceived flaws. They employ strategies such as becoming friends with your friends, turning them against you, manipulating you with gifts and rewards, and even bringing past mistakes back to haunt you. What they don't say is that they are afraid of you and that you can use the same tactics to get them. If you ever find yourself in a show with a manipulator, one of the best things you can do is turn the tables and beat them at their own game. This is true when you are forced to deal with a manipulator who is stealing your joy and making your life miserable, and you can no longer remain silent. Locate their centre of gravity—what makes them tick—and strike it. For example, if they have a unique skill, learn it and make it your own within the workplace. You can also become close to the people in power that he is close to, and if you are in a position of power, you can use your authority to recruit people with similar knowledge and skills. Such tactics usually throw a manipulator off balance and force him/her to refocus on their own life and career rather than yours.

• Have faith in your instincts and your judgement. Nobody can ever tell you what is best for you better than yourself. You may have noticed that many people seek second, third, or even fourth opinions on matters that are essentially their own. Manipulators see this as a potential loophole that they can take advantage of. When you begin looking for people's opinions, you give them a reason to define you. If, on the other hand, you have your own belief system, you can set firm boundaries that not even the manipulator can shake.

Relationship Manipulation

As previously stated, a manipulative person is someone who has mastered the art of deceiving others. Such people appear to be quite respectable, despite the fact that they are aware of how to calculate their moves in order to exploit someone else. It's a significant way for them to bring a stranger into their world while also ensuring that they're in an ensnare relationship with you. As a result, a manipulative person is known for having the courage to make critical decisions and take advantage of others. That being said, it's critical to address issues related to how such people draw others into their worlds in order to exploit them and delve into powerplay dockets that can ruin an individual. When it comes to starting a new relationship, most people aren't always sure what to expect, especially when it comes to character.

Manipulative people are well-known for taking others for a ride. Usually, the other party is completely committed to being truthful and not taking advantage of anyone else. However, in the real world, where people come in a variety of personalities, there are deceptive individuals who will always take advantage of others. Manipulative people have mastered the art of using their mental abilities to take advantage of others. They will appear to be respectful and loving at first, only to reveal their true intentions and devolve into deceptive traits that will harm the other party.

Having said that, powerplay in manipulation addresses the need for the other party to learn more about the manipulator's methods and take advantage of the situation at hand. As a result of powerplay in manipulation, the party that has been duped will learn more about how to reclaim that power and use it to their advantage. Powerplay is a strategy that allows the victim who was initially exploited to gain control. Powerplay is typically represented in various patterns that can be used by various people who have been trapped in the world of manipulative individuals at some point in their lives. As a result, it's critical to understand that powerplay in manipulation is all about finding a way out. It is critical for people to be aware of the most common powerplay that anyone else can use to get what they want back from people who have been manipulating them. This is true even when the argument appears to be one-sided.

There are several approaches to this, as you will see in the following chapters. Powerplay in manipulation occurs frequently when an individual twists what someone has said so that the message or information is barely recognisable to the person who said it. These people will try to perplex you by interrupting you or making you feel insane.

They will not only distort the truth, but will also tell lies as long as it serves their purposes. Furthermore, these same people will end up playing the victim and making an individual appear to be the ones who caused certain problems in another person's life. They may appear passive-aggressive and silent while feeling the need to prey on others. In powerplay, such people can appear nice at one point and then completely change their appearance in the next discussion. When they are attacked or legitimately questioned, they also become defensive and personal. They can delve into unique cases of people pursuing exactly what they want. Aside from that, these people may threaten you and, in many cases, refuse to let you go. This can be exhausting, especially when it comes to dealing with various issues that may be affecting a relationship.

Nonetheless, in powerplay, the person seeks to address personal vendetta in a variety of ways. There are additional characteristics that are added to how manipulative people can use powerplay to deceive others. It's critical to understand the issues that are linked to the problems so that you can avoid such people at all costs. It's also important to learn more about powerplay in order to recognise when someone is attempting to manipulate you. Staying alert allows you to stay true to yourself while making critical and viable decisions about how to move on and away from such people. With that said, it's also critical to commit to learning more about the fundamentals of powerplay in manipulation, as discussed in the following chapters. When it comes to dealing with the issues of a manipulative person, the first powerplay strategy is a lack of understanding about how other people tend to engage their friends and families while creating scenarios. This is also tied to the fact that people can truly believe in a certain way of handling a situation, as it may appear that their needs are being met. As a result, all existing situations and relationships, including what some people think and feel, are usually based on them. In the end, it doesn't really matter. Controllers and abusers do not seriously question their own character. They are unconcerned about the possibility that they are the source of the problem. Instead, they always claim that the looming problems are the fault of someone else. A manipulative person may also be unaware of other people's boundaries. As a result, they are not only relentless in their pursuit of what they want, but they also have no regard for getting along with other people. This implies that most manipulative people will cause harm to others along the way. Furthermore, such people lack understanding when it comes to crowding into someone else's space, not only physically but also emotionally. They do not fully internalise the importance of remaining focused when dealing with potentially personal issues. These people are easily compared to a tenacious parasite that seeks to remain attached to someone else who may be suffering as a result of being in such a relationship. Another powerplay strategy in manipulation occurs when a manipulator psychologically crowds your space.

The individual usually avoids accepting responsibility for any type of action that they may be in charge of. They might also continue to blame each other for causing it. As a result, it isn't that manipulative people are unaware that they are in charge of such duties and roles. However, they specifically choose to ignore the fundamentals and roots of dealing with such issues as they are required. They see nothing wrong with refusing to take on some of the duties and tasks that they intended to participate in and be responsible for. They also hold you liable for some of their actions. In the long run, these people may try to make you responsible for meeting the majority of their needs.

They also leave no room for the possibility of satisfying or fulfilling yours.

Aside from that, another powerplay strategy in manipulation is the use of one's mental ability to prey on the sensibilities or emotional sensitivity of others. This is especially true for those who have mastered the art of hooking you into a relationship that will drain you because you are kind, caring, and vulnerable in matters of the heart. Such people take advantage of the fact that you want to help them complete certain tasks or guide them through the process of becoming successful in a specific project. They will victimise you and take advantage of the fact that you are readily available to care for them regardless of your situation. They may also easily cater to the goodness of your heart in order to sweep you off your feet in the beginning. In the long run, the praise for such qualities will dwindle. They are only concerned with how you will serve them and nothing else. They are frequently easily persuaded that they can manipulate you by first drawing you to their side. Following that, they will use what they have learned about you to take advantage of you. Most of the time, these people act as if they care. In addition to the points you've gathered above, it's critical to always pay attention to the people with whom you interact. You can do this by paying attention to how they speak and how they interact with you. They will open up about how they are feeling about a topic. In other cases, they may gossip about you behind your back or insinuate something that is a red flag in a variety of ways. These people are also known as triangulation masters. They create dynamics that frequently allow for rivalry and jealousy. They both encourage and promote disharmony. To that end, you should never waste time attempting to explain yourself to them.

Manipulation is difficult to detect not only in relationships but also in character. This can range from being unconscious and subtle to being overt and calculated. Whatever the situation at the other end of the spectrum is, manipulation has a way of eroding a couple's bond and personal happiness. To make a relationship work, one must find a significant way to stay relevant in the team.

Manipulation has a way of turning people against you. This is due to the fact that it is largely the result of deception. To fully comprehend the pattern, including where it originated, it is critical to be able to recognise it yourself from the start of the relationship. That way, you'll be able to define your situation entirely, including how to proceed.

Manipulation Symptoms

Having said that, subtle Manipulation is known for appearing to involve well-meaning gestures that cause problems in the long run. As a result, the person in charge of manipulating others has no intention of causing you harm. He or she, on the other hand, will cause harm to another person without realising it. The intention of a manipulator is usually not to cause harm to another person. In many cases, it is motivated by the desire to be polite and non-confrontational. With time, these issues may be able to close off various lines of viable communication, leading to deeper looming issues. This is in addition to the fact that there are usually veiled attempts to obtain what someone desires.

This is true whether it is attached to love and approval, connection, or conflict avoidance in any way. Manipulation is always preceded by some form of guilt. If the person can persuade you to feel guilty about your actions even when you haven't done anything wrong, the individual will have a clear understanding of how easy it is to use you and ensure that you're convinced otherwise. A manipulator will make you feel their insecurities in various ways. This is usually done to see how they can control you in a variety of ways. For example, a person who has previously cheated on you will say that is why they do not want to have any male friends. This is typically a psychological strategy used to ensure that an individual feels safe to some extent.

Others may express regret for acting in a certain way.

As a result, when such people pinpoint some aspects of their lives, it is clear that they are using these issues to protect themselves from being caught up in these types of manipulative acts.

A manipulative person, on the other hand, is likely to make you doubt yourself in a variety of ways. Because your mind will be messed up, you will no longer be able to trust yourself. Such people will also consistently manipulate you while exaggerating your insecurities. They will use your current situation to your disadvantage. They will also constantly point out your flaws. These people will try to persuade you that they have your best interests at heart.

However, you should be cautious because they do not.

Conclusion

If you're here, it's obvious that you made it to the end of the book. Thank you for your interest in our book, Dark Manipulation: The Art of Dark Psychology, NLP Secrets, and Reading Body Language — Analyze Hidden Manipulative Behavior in Relationships and Take Control Using Different Mind Persuasion Techniques! We hope that the book provided you with an interesting and educational experience that you will remember. We also hope that the information you received here was beneficial and will assist you in achieving your goals and resolving any issues you may have had.

Now that you've finished the book, keep in mind that it's not the end of the road—keep reading to broaden your horizons!

The next step is to go out into the world and begin using the knowledge you gained from this book. If you require additional assistance beyond what the book provides, you should seek the advice of a mental health professional, as this information can only be backed up and supplemented with professional assistance. You'll be glad you did in any case.

Finally, keep in mind that some of the information in this book can be dangerous if used incorrectly. We repeatedly reminded the reader that the techniques discussed are powerful and should only be used for the right reasons and with the right people. Take care not to use any of the information provided to manipulate, dupe, or deceive others.